Understanding National Board Certification

Certification

A Guide for Teachers and Those Who Support Them

Mark W. Ellis

California State University, Fullerton

Tara Barnhart

California State University, Fullerton

Leslee M. Milch

Buena Park Elementary School District

Boston   Columbus   Indianapolis   New York   San Francisco   Upper Saddle River
Amsterdam   Cape Town   Dubai   London   Madrid   Milan   Munich   Paris   Montréal   Toronto
Delhi   Mexico City   São Paulo   Sydney   Hong Kong   Seoul   Singapore   Taipei   Tokyo

Senior Acquisitions Editor: *Kelly Villella Canton*
Editorial Assistant: *Annalea Manalili*
Executive Marketing Manager: *Krista Clark*
Senior Marketing Manager: Christine Gatchell
Production Editor: *Karen Mason*
Production Coordination and Electronic Composition: *Element LLC*
Text Design and Illustrations: *Element LLC*
Cover Designer: *Jenny Hart*
Cover Photo: *Exactostock/Superstock*
Photos: *Meiko Shimura, Teomara Rutherford, Kay Garcia*

Library of Congress Cataloging-in-Publication Data

CIP data unavailable at time of publication.

10 9 8 7 6 5 4 3 2 1

ISBN 10: 0-13-210137-8
ISBN 13: 978-0-13-210137-0

About the Authors

Mark W. Ellis, PhD, NBCT, is an associate professor of secondary education at California State University, Fullerton. Prior to earning his PhD in education from the University of North Carolina, Chapel Hill, Mark taught mathematics in Grades 6–12 in northern California public schools for six years, becoming a National Board Certified Teacher in Early Adolescence Mathematics in 1999 (and renewing in 2009). Mark's professional work focuses on supporting preservice and experienced teachers in creating opportunities for all students—particularly those from groups historically underserved by traditional practices of schooling—to make sense of important mathematics concepts and skills. He helped establish the Professional Teaching Development Center at CSU Fullerton in 2008, which coordinated National Board candidate outreach and support for teachers across four Southern California counties. His work has been published in numerous journals including *Teachers College Record, Learning Environments Research*, and *Mathematics Teacher,* and his ongoing work with teachers of mathematics in high-need schools has received generous funding from the National Science Foundation (NSF). He was the editor of the book *Mathematics for All: Responding to Diversity, Grades 6–8*, published by the National Council of Teachers of Mathematics (NCTM) in 2008, and currently serves on the NCTM Board of Directors (2011–2014).

Tara Barnhart, MA, NBCT, taught high school science for 13 years in the Whittier Union High School District, where she earned National Board Certification and served as a mentor teacher. Since 2007 she has been a full-time lecturer in secondary education at CSU Fullerton. Her responsibilities include teaching the introductory course on National Board Certification for master's students and teaching in the science credential program. She also serves as the director of CSU Fullerton's National Board support program. Tara is pursuing her PhD in education at UC Irvine. She has presented her research on teacher reflection and classroom discourse at state, national, and international conferences.

Leslee M. Milch, MS, NBCT, is a reading specialist with 18 years experience teaching kindergarten, first, and second grade limited English proficiency (LEP) students in the Buena Park Elementary School District in Orange County, California. She has also served as the district's Beginning Teacher Support and Assessment Induction Program coordinator. Since certifying as an NBCT in 2003, Leslee has served as a candidate support provider (CSP) and the recruitment/outreach coordinator with the Orange County Department of Education's National Board Candidate Support Program. She currently is a member of the California State University, Fullerton National Board Certification Advisory Board and works as a CSP with the National Board Candidate support program at CSU Fullerton. Leslee is an NBPTS faculty member, and in this capacity facilitates CSP training seminars across the country. As an NBCT State Farm Liaison and the Boeing Ambassador program coordinator with NBPTS, Leslee has served as an education advocate and spokesperson at the local, state, and national levels. Currently, Leslee is a member of the NBPTS Early Childhood Generalist Standards Committee working to revise these certificate standards.

Contents

Foreword

It is my pleasure to write the Foreword for this book because our students are deserving of the best possible educators who will provide them with experiences needed to realize their fullest potential. This book offers educators a detailed look at the National Board for Professional Teaching Standards (NBPTS) and how you can most productively engage in the process necessary to earn National Board Certification. Powerfully, the authors speak from first-hand experience as candidates and from their work with candidates about how this process is more about professional transformation than simply professional recognition.

Being an educator cannot be viewed as a stagnant profession. Just in the past two decades, major changes have occurred in recommended practice for how we approach teaching and learning including changes in content, in national and state standards, in the technology to access information and communicate with one another, and in the knowledge and skills needed to be effective with the youth of today. As educators we must adjust and modify our practice, continuing to learn and becoming even more effective in providing all students with the instructional experiences, knowledge, and passion that will prepare them with the tools to reach their goals in life.

In my experience as a teacher educator, I found that my teacher candidates moved through a three-stage process as they became experienced and capable teachers, what these authors describe as high-impact teachers. During their novice stage, they reflected *on* practice using the instructional strategies and observations from their teacher training experiences. In their intermediate stage, they reflected *in* practice, learning from past practice and using that knowledge to modify instruction. As they became strong and skilled teachers, they developed a vision of what they wanted their students to learn and how they could effectively accomplish that vision. During this stage, they were using reflection *for* practice, moving from maintaining to having the skills and knowledge of what they needed to do to be effective teachers. These teachers continually grew as professionals and had the greatest impact on student learning and development. The National Board Certification process and its emphasis on using evidence from students to inform decision making as educators provides an excellent model for supporting teachers in reflecting *for* practice.

With the help of this book, you will understand the NBPTS certification process is teacher led, teacher created, and teacher defined; and you will learn that it is a process grounded in the idea of professional growth as a continual cycle. Importantly, as the authors make clear, you will get the most from this process if you go through the journey with colleagues. In doing so, you will expand and deepen your professional relationships and more clearly recognize the responsibility we have as educators to work collaboratively to improve learning for all students.

In closing, I would like to share with you a story about Kathleen Parker, recipient of the 2010 Pulitzer Prize for commentary. In a *Washington Post* column written shortly after winning the Pulitzer, she described how her 11th grade English teacher, by extending an imaginary sprig of verbena, introduced her to William Faulkner.

She called him the light master and holds him with distinction because he changed her life with a flicker of light. As an insecure adolescent in a new school with unfamiliar classmates, Kathleen remembers being called on to identify some part of a sentence her teacher had written on the blackboard, not knowing the answer, and being showered with the laughter of her classmates. Embarrassed and wanting to hide under her desk, at that instant her teacher tossed her a lifesaver in the form of a swift and public rebuke of her peers. In no uncertain terms he told the class to stop laughing because Kathleen was a stellar writer who could out-write them all. She marks that day as her birth as a writer. Almost 20 years later, Kathleen went back to visit her teacher, Mr. Gasque, who at first did not remember her. When she recounted her tale of being saved from ridicule, he invited her to stay to talk with his class. After she completed the talk, a teary Mr. Gasque held out some worn sheets of lined paper on which she found an essay she had written so long ago on Faulkner's book, "The Unvanquished." (http://www.washingtonpost.com/wp-dyn/content/article/2010/04/13/AR2010041303683.html)

Turning on the lights moves us to *hope*—the hope that every child, every student will have a teacher who as a light master dramatically impacts his or her life of learning. I expect that many of those teachers will be National Board Certified Teachers.

Carol E. Malloy, Ph.D. is Professor Emeritus, University of North Carolina at Chapel Hill. She is proud to have taught mathematics in urban middle and high schools for 20 years before moving into teacher education. Carol has been active in the Benjamin Banneker Association since 1991 and served as its president from 1996–1998. She was elected to the National Council of Teachers of Mathematics Board of Directors (1998–2002) and was a member of the NCTM Standards 2000 writing team. Carol chaired the NBPTS Adolescence and Young Adulthood Mathematics Standards Revision Committee and in 2009 received the UNC Chapel Hill Mentor Award for Lifetime Achievement.

Preface

This book is written by, for, and about those who have chosen to live their professional lives as teachers. The National Board for Professional Teaching Standards (NBTPS; **www.nbpts.org**), through its rigorous performance-based assessment created by panels of expert educators, exemplifies the highest standards of our profession. Those who meet these standards earn advanced certification that is nationally recognized as an indicator of professional excellence. Please note that we use the term *teacher* throughout this book in the broadest possible sense to include education professionals of all positions, including speech therapists, counselors, language specialists, and classroom teachers.

It is our belief that every teacher can benefit from learning about the National Board standards and participating in the National Board Certification process. We know of no better way to learn about yourself as a professional than to engage in this process that is grounded in reflecting on evidence of how what you know and do every day impacts student learning. Simply put, the National Board Certification process is one of the most effective professional learning experiences available for teachers. Rather than something to *get through*, it is something to *grow from*. This belief is what led each of us to pursue the challenge of certification and is why we decided to support other educators through the process. It is also what led us to write this book—we sincerely hope this resource serves you well along your journey toward National Board Certification and/or helps you in your support of others in their pursuit of this professional milestone.

The Purpose of This Book

This book is a guide for teachers looking to enhance their growth as education professionals, in particular through the process of National Board Certification. Although NBPTS does provide instructions about the candidate assessment process, this book goes beyond those logistics to really dig into understanding what it means to look for evidence of student learning that results from what you know and do every day, reflect on your professional knowledge and practice, and write about the insights that emerge from such efforts. Because earning National Board Certification is not about completing a checklist of activities, a cookie-cutter "how-to" guide would be inappropriate. Instead, we have spent time laying the groundwork for how candidates can meaningfully engage with each aspect of the certification process. Our own experiences as candidates and providing support to candidates have contributed to the content and character of this book. Reflecting on this work, we have included information about how candidates can get the most from their efforts to complete the portfolio entries and assessment center exercises, whether individually or within collaborative cohorts, as well as ideas for those who work with candidates about how to most productively provide such support.

The Audience of This Book

Educators who understand that their work as professionals is an ongoing cycle of reflection and growth will appreciate the perspectives we offer in this book. Whether you are contemplating one slice of the National Board assessment process through *Take One!,* pursuing the full candidate portfolio and assessment center, continuing your journey toward certification as a retake or advanced candidate, or thinking about renewing your National Board Certification, you will find information and ideas within these pages that are timely, useful, and tested. For those who provide candidate support, this book will provide you with additional perspectives and research-based strategies to make your work even more effective. Finally, we strongly encourage anyone with an interest in understanding the professional work of teachers to read this book and consider what goes into creating learning environments that support every student in working toward her or his full potential.

Key Features of This Book

We have incorporated some key features throughout this book that warrant pointing out. First and foremost is our effort to provide connections to research that supports the standards of NBPTS and provides insights into your work as a candidate for National Board Certification. In most every chapter you will find references to research that we've used to generate the ideas and advice we provide. While certainly our own experiences as National Board Certified Teachers and candidate support providers have informed our thinking as well, we felt it important to let readers know the research base that supports this process. Full references are at the end of the book should you wish to follow up on a particular citation.

Each chapter includes comments from NBCTs and candidates we've worked with over the years. We hope you find their insights helpful; sometimes knowing others shared some of the same anxieties you feel during the assessment process can be reassuring.

The official portfolio instructions from NBPTS include tools to help organize your thinking. Knowing that teachers more often adapt resources rather than adopt them, we've included several tools of our own. Some we've modified from those offered by NBPTS based on our experience with candidates. Others are tools we've created to provide additional support for the thinking, writing, and organizing the National Board Certification process requires. Examples of completed forms are provided when the NBPTS ethical guidelines permit.

Although we think all the information in this book is important, this symbol is used to draw attention to particular points. These are typically common misconceptions or potential sources of problems candidates have or experience during the National Board process.

Finally, we realize that answering one question often leads to the asking of many more. At the end of each chapter, space is provided for you to jot down any reflections that come to mind as you process the ideas shared or questions posed in the chapter. In addition, many of the chapters include a list of additional resources should you want to explore further the ideas we touch on in the text.

Whether or not you are familiar with National Board Certification, we encourage you to read Chapter 1, which provides an overview of how NBPTS was established. It is important that you have a clear sense of the history and the mission of the organization. Once you're ready to move into the certification process, take a look at the section that follows. We have organized an at-a-glance overview by candidate type (i.e., *Take One!* candidate, full certification candidate, retake or advanced candidate, and renewal candidate) as a way to give you a quick look at what will be required of you and guide you to the parts of this book most relevant to the goal toward which you are working.

Take One! Candidate

As a *Take One!* candidate, you will complete one predetermined classroom-based portfolio entry that involves an examination of your impact on student learning and development and is supported by a video of your practice. This is a way to gradually introduce yourself to the National Board process; it's like dipping your toe in to test the water rather than jumping in all at once. Anyone with access to a classroom of students can participate in *Take One!* Those pursuing *Take One!* should read the following chapters:

- Chapter 1: Introduction to National Board Certification
- Chapter 2: Understanding the Standards
- Chapter 3: Getting Started (including sections on ethical guidelines, first month's checklist, essential steps and organizational tips for all candidates, entry planning including overall considerations and planning for the video-based entries)
- Chapter 4: Thinking, Dialoguing, and Writing About Teaching
- Chapter 5: Looking for Evidence of the Standards (all sections *except* the one on documented accomplishments entry)
- Chapter 6: Sending Your Portfolio: Packing the Box

Once you've submitted the one required portfolio entry, Chapter 8, Planning for Score Release, is recommended reading in November as you prepare for the results you'll receive by December 31 (but typically in early December).

Full Certification Candidate

As a full candidate for National Board Certification, you will complete four written portfolio entries that provide evidence of your professional practices and their impact on student learning and development and complete six assessment center tasks that provide evidence of your content knowledge and pedagogical knowledge. You must have at least three years of experience working as a fully credentialed teacher in order to be eligible for full certification. If you are unsure whether you meet this requirement, call 1-800-22-TEACH (1-800-228-3224) to have NBPTS review your particular status. If you are a candidate for full certification, you should read the following chapters to help you through the entire process:

- Chapter 1: Introduction to National Board Certification
- Chapter 2: Understanding the Standards

- Chapter 3: Getting Started (don't miss the Full Candidate Quick Tips table, Table 3.2, p. 30.).
- Chapter 4: Thinking, Dialoguing, and Writing About Teaching
- Chapter 5: Looking for Evidence of the Standards
- Chapter 6: Sending Your Portfolio: Packing the Box
- Chapter 7: Preparing for the Assessment Center

Once you've submitted the portfolio and completed the assessment center, Chapter 8, Planning for Score Release, is recommended reading in November as you prepare for the results you'll receive by December 31 (but typically in early December).

Retake or Advanced Candidate

As a retake or advanced candidate, your first task is to identify what entry (or entries) and/or exercises you will be retaking. Once you've done so, use the following information to determine the chapters and sections that will be most relevant for you:

- We strongly recommend you (re)read Chapter 2, Understanding the Standards, as a way to get your head back into the NBPTS mind-set.
- Read relevant sections of Chapter 3, Getting Started, and don't miss the Retake Candidate Quick Tips table, Table 3.3, p. 30.
- If you will be retaking any of the portfolio entries, be sure to use Chapter 4, Thinking, Dialoguing, and Writing About Teaching; Chapter 5, Looking for Evidence of the Standards (all relevant sections); and Chapter 6, Sending Your Portfolio: Packing the Box.
- If you will be retaking any of the assessment center exercises, read Chapter 7, Preparing for the Assessment Center.
- Once you've submitted the portfolio entry (or entries) and/or completed the assessment center exercise(s) you selected to retake, Chapter 8, Planning for Score Release, is recommended reading in November as you prepare for the results you'll receive by December 31 (but typically in early December).

Renewal Candidate

Having earned certification once, the renewal process is meant more as a status check than as another hurdle to clear; this is a "pass/no pass" process rather than one based on earning a specific number of points. NBPTS wants to know what you've done in order to grow professionally as an educator and impact student learning in the years since becoming National Board certified. We strongly encourage you to consider renewal! If your certificate lapses, you will need to go through the entire portfolio and assessment processes if you later decide to recertify. It is recommended you read the following chapters and sections as you prepare for and engage in the renewal process, referred to as compiling a Profile of Professional Growth (PPG):

- We strongly recommend you (re)read Chapter 2, Understanding the Standards, as a way to get yourself back into the NBPTS mind-set.

- Read relevant sections of Chapter 3, Getting Started, and don't miss the Renewal Candidate Quick Tips table, Table 3.4, p. 31.
- If it's been awhile since you've engaged in reflective writing (though we know you reflect on your work all the time), read through Chapter 4, Thinking, Dialoguing, and Writing About Teaching.
- And last but certainly not least, read the section of Chapter 9, You've Earned National Board Certification: Now What?, that is all about renewal!

CourseSmart eBook and other eBook Options Available

CourseSmart is an exciting new choice for purchasing this book. As an alternative to purchasing the printed book, you may purchase an electronic version of the same content via CourseSmart for reading on PC, MAC, as well as Android devices, iPad, iPhone and iPod Touch with CourseSmart Apps. With a CourseSmart eBook, readers can search the text, make notes online, print out reading assignments that incorporate lecture notes, and bookmark important passages for later review. For more information or to purchase access to the CourseSmart eBook, visit **http://www. coursesmart.com http://www.coursesmart.com/**. Also look for availability of this book on a number of other eBook devices and platforms.

Acknowledgments

This book would not have been possible without the outstanding teachers and students we have had the privilege to work with and learn from during our many years as educators and candidate support providers. Our own work in classrooms has taught us that children of all ages are capable of amazing insights and accomplishments when given the support to grow and learn. And our work with teachers has motivated us beyond measure; that so many professionals who already put in 110 percent each week in their classrooms were willing to find time on nights and weekends to allow us to accompany them along their journey toward National Board Certification has been truly inspiring. Furthermore, the National Board Certified Teachers and candidate support providers who took time to provide feedback on earlier drafts of this book provided invaluable insights that certainly improved the quality of our writing.

Over the many years that California State University, Fullerton has offered National Board candidate support we have been fortunate to receive excellent support ourselves from NBPTS largely due to the efforts of Linda Manuel, former NBPTS regional outreach coordinator for southern California. We would be remiss if we did not thank our editor, Kelly Villella Canton, whose belief in our ability to actually write this book and whose supportive feedback along the way toward publication helped our idea become a reality. We would like to thank all of the reviewers who read our preliminary manuscript and provided comments that helped us to clarify our thinking and make the book more user-friendly: Ronarae Adams, National University; Robin Atwood, University of Southern Mississippi; Barb Baltrinic, The University of Akron; Patty Fay Dimetres, Fairfax County Public Schools; Debra Dosemagen, Mount Mary College; Beth Edwards, North Carolina Department of Public Instruction; Terri Foughty, Newcastle

Public Schools; Marci J. Gonzalez, Othello High School; Julie Kang, University of Washington; Suzanne Martinez, National-Louis University; Debra Pastore, Washington State University; Jason A. Schmid, Oak Harbor Middle School; and Carrie Usui Johnson, UCLA Center X.

Finally, we want to offer our gratitude to our families, friends, and loved ones whose support and understanding throughout the writing process gave us the encouragement and energy to complete this project. In particular, Mark thanks his co-authors, his mentor Carol Malloy, his parents Kay and Bill Ellis, and his partner in life Meiko Shimura for their constant support and encouragement. Tara wishes to thank her co-authors, as well as Roberta Berg, Victoria Costa, Beth van Es, and Freda Ross for their wisdom and guidance. Appreciation abounds for Emily and Ethan, who amaze her every day. Leslee wishes to thank her mentor and biggest supporter in life, Mom Warne. She thanks her co-authors for their spirit of collaboration and commitment to National Board candidates. And her greatest appreciation is extended to all her students and their families, who have touched her life in so many ways over the years.

Introduction to National Board Certification®

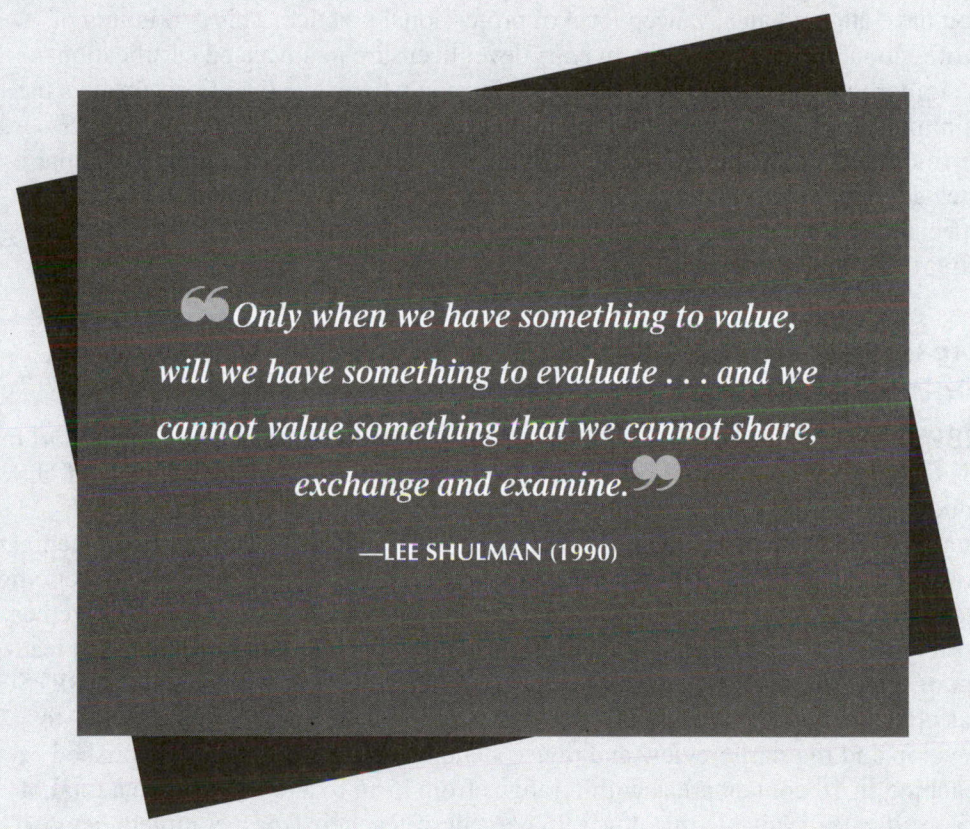

> 66 *Only when we have something to value,*
> *will we have something to evaluate . . . and we*
> *cannot value something that we cannot share,*
> *exchange and examine.* 99
>
> —LEE SHULMAN (1990)

As a professional within the field of education you are passionate about and committed to the work you do and its impact on the learners with whom you work. The National Board for Professional Teaching Standards (NBPTS; **www.nbpts.org**) is a nonprofit organization created from this same passion and commitment with the aim of identifying and advancing accomplished professional practice in education. This chapter will provide you with background information about NBPTS, its certification process, and research about the impact of National Board Certification on teachers and their students. As mentioned in the Preface, we use the term *teacher* throughout this book in the broadest possible sense to include those working in a variety of roles, including speech therapists, counselors, language specialists, and classroom teachers. There are National Board certificate standards for each of these categories of education professionals.

From Initial Licensure to Advanced Certification

Teaching is a profession. This simple statement acknowledges that teachers are members of a community where professional standards exist for both obtaining *initial licensure* and identifying *expert practice*. At the entry level, individuals who meet their state standards for becoming a licensed teacher are frequently referred to as "highly qualified." This terminology comes from the No Child Left Behind (NCLB) legislation of 2001. While symbolizing that you have met a strict set of minimum standards for entering the teaching profession, being highly qualified is a starting point from which to enter the profession. As you gain experience and insight, you will seek opportunities to continue your professional growth and development. The National Board assessment process is an opportunity to demonstrate you have attained an advanced level of professional practice. This continuum of professional development—from entry-level licensure to advanced certification—is similar to that found in the medical profession where "medical licensure sets the minimum competency requirements to diagnose and treat patients," whereas "Board certification . . . demonstrate[s] a physician's exceptional expertise in a particular specialty and/or subspecialty of medical practice" (American Board of Medical Specialties, 2009). If earning a teaching license is a starting point, then how is expert teaching practice recognized?

Creation of the National Board for Professional Teaching Standards

NBPTS was established in 1987 in response to the recommendations of a report by the Carnegie Forum on Education and the Economy (1986) about the state of U.S. education and the need to create a rigorous set of standards to recognize high-quality "accomplished" teaching. Organized as an independent, nongovernmental, nonprofit organization, NBPTS is led by a board comprised primarily of practicing classroom teachers (who are required to form a majority of its members) together with university teacher educators, subject matter experts, policy makers, and leaders of educational organizations. During its more than 20-year existence, NBPTS has convened panels of experts—classroom teachers and university faculty—to develop and regularly review and revise standards for certifying accomplished teaching in 16 content areas within ranges from birth to age 18 to make a total of 25 certificates available that cover 95 percent of teachers (for a complete list visit **www.nbpts.org/for_candidates**).

Modeled after advanced "board certification" practices within the medical profession, NBPTS has three primary goals that define its mission:

1. To maintain high and rigorous standards for what accomplished teachers should know and be able to do.
2. To provide a national voluntary system for certifying teachers who meet these standards.
3. To capitalize on the expertise of National Board Certified Teachers (NBCTs).[1]

---

[1]From NBPTS, *Mission Statement*, retrieved from **http://www.nbpts.org/about_us/mission_and_history/mission**.

As of 2011 there were over 97,000 NBCTs in the United States, roughly 3 percent of the overall teacher population (though this percentage varies from one state to another).

Overview of the National Board Certification Process

Unlike state licensing requirements, which certify that you have met the minimum requirements, National Board standards are a measure of advanced certification. For that reason, only licensed teachers with at least three years' teaching experience are eligible to apply for board certification. However, the *Take One!* option allows both experienced teachers and those with less than three years' teaching experience (including student teachers as well as those not in the classroom, such as administrators) to participate in one component of the portfolio process.

According to the National Board (2002), effective teachers possess five main characteristics that hold true across all content areas and developmental age groups. These Five Core Propositions, which will be explored in more depth in Chapter 2, form the essence of the National Board Standards and underpin all that NBPTS does. The Five Core Propositions are:[2]

1. Teachers are committed to students and their learning.
2. Teachers know the subjects they teach and how to teach those subjects to students.
3. Teachers are responsible for managing and monitoring student learning.
4. Teachers think systematically about their practice and learn from experience.
5. Teachers are members of learning communities.

   (National Board for Professional Teaching Standards [NBPTS], 2002, pp. 3–4)

Effective teaching is also defined by the demonstration of certificate standards that have been established by committees of teachers and experts in subject matter content, child development, assessment, and higher education. Built upon the foundation of these Five Core Propositions, certificate standards are both content-specific and developmental age-specific. This is a model of professional practice created by and for teachers, not imposed by those external to the real work of teaching. As such, you will find that the descriptions of accomplished practice, while setting the bar high, speak to the heart of why you went into the education profession and reflect what you know and do every day.

Both the Core Propositions and accompanying certificate standards interact and are put into practice in a model called the Architecture of Accomplished Teaching that involves a cycle of goal setting, planning, enactment, reflection, and revision. This cycle can take place in the course of a single day of instruction, over the course of an instructional sequence, or over the course of a semester or school year. While you can find out more about this model in NBPTS candidate materials, Chapter 2 will offer you a similar model we've created, the Cycle of High Impact Teaching, to help you think about how these processes are related to the certification process.

The degree to which your practice reflects the Five Core Propositions, the certificate standards, and the processes within the Architecture of Accomplished Teaching is measured through completion of a two-part assessment: the portfolio

---

[2]Reprinted with permission from the National Board for Professional Teaching Standards, **www.nbpts.org**. All rights reserved.

and the assessment center. The full candidate portfolio consists of four entries, each focusing on different aspects of your professional practice. Typically, three of these entries require you to document and analyze evidence of the impact of your work with current students. These entries might include evidence of using assessment over time to monitor student learning and inform teacher practice; evidence of specific pedagogical practices and student work samples demonstrating their effectiveness; and videos of teacher–student and/or student–student interactions. A fourth portfolio entry requires the documentation and analysis of professional practices and accomplishments that demonstrate how you go beyond the scope of what is expected in your everyday work, both within and outside the school setting, to impact student learning.

The portfolio requirements are specific to each certificate and are available on the National Board website. The four portfolio entries are typically due to be submitted in March of the certification cycle year in which they were started (though you should always check for the deadlines specific to the cycle in which you have applied).

Whereas the primary focus of the portfolio is pedagogical practice, the assessment center is designed to measure both the depth and breadth of your content knowledge. Required of only full candidates, the assessment center consists of responding to six different prompts, one at a time, within a fixed time period. Like the portfolio entries, each assessment center exercise is specific to both the content area and developmental age range of the certificate being sought. There may also be some interplay of content knowledge and pedagogy—what Shulman (1987) refers to as pedagogical content knowledge—in the assessment center exercises. This assessment is taken at a private testing center (see **www.nbpts.org** for a list of centers closest to you) in the spring or summer of the certification cycle year. Once you check in at your testing center, you will be seated in front of a computer and presented with one prompt at a time and given 30 minutes to type your response to each one. As with the portfolio instructions, the areas of focus for the assessment center prompts are available on the National Board website.

Following submission, the four portfolio entries and responses to the six assessment center prompts are then separated and sent to be blind-scored at centers around the country. National Board assessors are trained in scoring just 1 of the 10 components and must be practicing, licensed teachers both in the subject and developmental age corresponding to the certificate entry they are evaluating. Each entry is scored separately by multiple assessors using rubrics developed by committees of trained teacher-assessors. Candidates earning a total of at least 275 points are deemed to have met the standards of accomplished teaching and therefore achieve National Board Certification.

It is important to know that National Board Certification is viewed by NBPTS as a professional growth experience that may take one to three years to complete, with significant and lasting impacts on teaching practices and student learning for those who persist and work to meet the standards established for effective practice. For this reason, candidates earning less than 275 points in their first attempt at certification are encouraged to "bank" their scores from stronger entries and "retake" other entries over the course of the next two certification cycles. The National Board refers to this as "retake candidacy" (also "advanced candidacy"), and specific portions of this book are designed for retake candidates. Note that in order to have a valid score generated, candidates for full certification must submit all four portfolio entries and all six assessment center exercises during the initial attempt to certify; those whose scores are less than 275 will then have two additional certification cycles during which to work toward meeting or exceeding 275 points.

For those who do not yet meet the eligibility requirements to become a candidate for full certification (hold an undergraduate degree; hold a valid teaching credential in the state in which they are teaching; completed three years of teaching as a fully credentialed teacher), or who are interested in National Board Certification but are not yet ready to commit to full candidacy, the *Take One!* option is available. *Take One!* requires participants to complete and submit one preselected portfolio entry. Although the entry selected varies from certificate to certificate, it always requires the analysis of a video of your classroom teaching and interaction as well as supporting instructional materials. Once submitted, this entry is scored along with all the other entries within the same certificate area submitted by full candidates, and scores are reported at the same time as those for full candidates. *Take One!* participants who achieve a raw score of 2.75 or higher may choose to bank their score and apply it toward full candidacy within the next three certification cycles (three years). Specific portions of this book are designed for *Take One!* participants.

Once earned, National Board Certification is valid for 10 years. If as an NBCT you choose to renew certification, you become a "renewal candidate" during either years 8 to 9 or 9 to 10 of your certification. The renewal process consists of one submission with three components analyzing the impact of Professional Growth Experiences (PGEs) that you have selected and a reflection on these PGEs. At least one 10-minute video of you teaching in your certificate area is required. Portions of this book are designed specifically for renewal candidates. Please note that NBCTs who allow their certification to lapse are not eligible for the renewal process and must instead complete the entire 10-entry process again.

> **"***I am a better teacher because of this process. I know that an accomplished teacher has the greatest impact on student learning. Most importantly, I realize that I have a lot more to learn. I'm still growing [as a professional].***"**
>
> —NBCT, LITERACY: READING/LANGUAGE ARTS

Why Pursue National Board Certification?

With all of the demands on your time—lesson planning, evaluation of student work, conferences and parent communication, meetings (not to mention your personal life)—why try to squeeze in one more thing? While the answer to this question will be different for each person reading this book, among the many responses given, we usually hear teachers express one or more of the following reasons for pursuing National Board Certification:

- Examining one's practices against the highest standards of professional practice
- Experiencing professional development intensely focused on the everyday work of teaching
- Becoming even more effective at impacting student learning
- Earning the ability to teach in over 40 states without additional requirements
- Joining a national cadre of teacher leaders whose voices impact education policy
- Making oneself more desirable to school districts
- Having a greater possibility of being immune from staffing reductions

- Earning higher salaries
- Experiencing the stimulation of regular, productive dialogue about the craft of teaching with like-minded colleagues

A Professionally Rewarding Experience

Surveys and interviews with teachers who have been through the National Board assessment process have found widespread agreement that, although it is certainly a rigorous performance assessment, it is also a professional development experience without compare (Cohen & Rice, 2005; Lustick & Sykes, 2006). Teachers who have been through the assessment process report becoming more refined in their assessment practices, tying routine assessment to lesson planning and curriculum design, and better connecting students' experiences and prior knowledge with what is being learned. This is the result of having to provide evidence—clear, consistent, and convincing—that demonstrates how one's professional practices meet the rigorous National Board standards in the certificate area being pursued accompanied by reflective narrative that shows an awareness of one's strengths and areas for further growth as a teacher who significantly impacts student development and learning.

Each of us authors can state unequivocally that due to the National Board assessment process our teaching became not only more effective but more efficient! While we might have felt initially that working toward National Board Certification was a way to see whether our level of expertise as professionals measured up to national standards of excellence, we soon learned that the process itself would require us to look deeply into our teaching practices and question whether and how well these met our students' developmental and learning needs. Through the intense analysis and reflection required of candidates, we found ways to improve our work by identifying those actions that truly impact student development and learning. As a result we developed a more finely focused perspective on our own practice as teachers that enabled us to make better instructional decisions and implement teaching practices to make the best use of our time with students.

Nationwide, National Board Certification is regarded as the highest level of teacher accomplishment and, as such, is accepted by almost every state as equivalent to full licensure in the certificate area. This means an NBCT is able to move from one state to another without the burden of additional licensing requirements. For up-to-date information about each state's position on reciprocity for National Board Certification, contact the appropriate state department of education.

In addition to reciprocity, many states and local school districts have placed bonuses or incentives for NBCTs into their teacher salary schedules. For example, for many years North Carolina offered NBCTs a 12 percent pay increase, an incentive that contributed to the state leading the nation with 10 percent of its teachers having earned National Board Certification! The National Board maintains a web page with information about state and local incentives: **www.nbpts.org/resources/state_local_information**. It is always a good idea, however, to check with your state office of education and local school district for current incentive information, as these can and do change.

Finally, many states and districts consider National Board Certification an additional qualification one has earned and in some cases use it as an additional criterion when making staffing decisions. In an increasingly competitive hiring environment, it is an excellent idea to set yourself apart by earning the highest level of certification possible.

A Process Supported by Research

Research on the National Board assessment process and of NBCTs has identified several significant effects related to teacher professional development, student learning and achievement, and teacher retention. Lustick and Sykes (2006) examined the National Board assessment process as a form of professional development by interviewing three cohorts of National Board candidates. They found that as a result of the process, teachers learned "to evaluate their own practice in the light of objective, external standards" (Lustick & Sykes, 2006, p. 29). The professional gains for teachers, moreover, were found for all candidates regardless of whether they attained National Board Certification. As most candidates will attest, the certification process itself is professionally meaningful.

In a thorough review of data and prior research on National Board Certification, the National Research Council (Hakel, Koenig, & Elliott, 2008) found strong evidence that students of NBCTs benefit in a myriad of ways. Given recent attention to the issue of teacher quality, it is important that multiple measures are used that capture a broad picture of all that teachers know and do. Hakel, Koenig, and Elliott (2008) draw parallels to professionals in other fields to point out the problems inherent in looking at only one type of outcome to evaluate teacher impact:

> Measures of outcomes for students, such as their academic achievement, do provide a means of evaluating teachers' job performance, but there are some drawbacks to the use of this kind of a criterion measure. It is enlightening to consider what this would mean if extrapolated to other fields. For example, this is similar to evaluating the validity of a medical certification test by collecting information about the outcomes for patients of a board-certified physician or evaluating the validity of the bar exam by considering the outcomes for clients of a lawyer who had passed the bar exam and been admitted to the bar. Outcomes for patients reflect many factors other than the skills and knowledge of the physician who provides services, such as the severity of the illness being treated and the degree to which the patient adheres to the professional advice given. Likewise in law, the outcome for the client depends on such factors as the nature of the legal problem, the record of prior legal problems, and the extent to which the client follows the advice. (p. 25)

Understanding that using standardized achievement tests as a measure of teacher impact on student outcomes is far from perfect, research on NBCTs nonetheless has found evidence that "National Board Certification distinguishes more effective teachers from less effective teachers with respect to student achievement" (Hakel et al., 2008, p. 179). Additionally, students of NBCTs show greater academic gains and exhibit better writing and critical thinking skills than the students of their non-NBCT colleagues.

Broadening the perspective to examine other forms of student outcomes, Bond, Smith, Baker, and Hattie (2000) examined classroom practices and student work samples of NBCTs and non-NBCTs. Using classroom observations the researchers rated the lessons across 13 dimensions of accomplished teaching and found lessons of NBCTs to be more highly rated than lessons of non-NBCTs on 11 of these. Particularly powerful is their finding that "74 percent of the work samples of students taught by NBCTs reflected deep understanding, while 29 percent of the work samples of non-NBCTs were judged to reflect deep understanding" (in Hakel et al., 2008, p. 279).

Lending further evidence as to the validity of National Board Certification as an indicator of expert practice, Berliner (2004) examined 12 measures of expertise among a group of teachers who all attempted National Board Certification. It was found that on all 12 measures teachers who certified outperformed teachers who did not certify. In addition, significant differences in the quality of student work samples were found between NBCTs and non-NBCTs.

With respect to the relationship between board certification and a teacher's career pathway, studies have found that NBCTs remain in the profession longer and demonstrate increased collegiality and leadership. This is important since the recruitment and retention of teachers is a critical issue in education, particularly in schools serving high-need populations. Keeping highly effective teachers in our nation's schools by recognizing their expert level of professional practice is imperative to the quality of not only educational opportunities offered in their classrooms but also peer mentoring and leadership they can provide to colleagues.

Questions to Ask Yourself

Now that you know more about the origins of National Board Certification, the certification process, and the research that supports it, it is a good time to ask yourself what is leading you to consider pursuing National Board Certification. It is important that you take time to carefully consider the reasons for this because the process will require a high level of commitment and effort. Some questions to ask yourself include:

- What led me into teaching?
- What is it that keeps me in the profession?
- What will it mean to me, personally and professionally, to earn National Board Certification?
- What forms of support—professional and personal—will I have (or need) as I go through the assessment process?
- Where am I professionally with regard to my teaching practice? And what is my ability to commit my time and effort to this process? Is *Take One!* a good place to begin this journey, or am I ready to pursue full certification?

❝I pursued National Board certification because I knew it was a vehicle where I could completely dissect and evaluate my own teaching practices to make sure I was fostering the best possible learning experience in my classroom.❞

—NBCT, LITERACY: READING/LANGUAGE ARTS

It is our hope that your responses to these questions will help guide you as you consider your readiness for entering into what will be a transformational journey toward certification. We've summarized the certification pathways in Figure 1.1 to make it easier for you to see the requirements for *Take One!*, full certification, and renewal. There is space for you to record your thoughts following this (and every) chapter, and we encourage you to take a moment to do so. The remaining chapters are designed to provide support for you as you go through this process of professional growth and

FIGURE 1.1

National Board Certification Pathways

Take One! (optional)	
Open to anyone with access to a class of students including student teachers, credentialed teachers, and administrators.	Consists of 1 portfolio entry involving video and reflection on student outcomes. Scores can be applied to full certification for the next three certification cycles (three years).

Full Certification	
Open to educators with an undergraduate degree and at least three years' experience as a fully credentialed professional.	Initial attempt requires 4 portfolio entries and 6 assessment center exercises. A score of 275 or greater is needed to earn certification. If score is less than 275, strongest entries can be "banked" and other entries retaken during the next two certification cycles.

Renewal	
National Board Certification is valid for 10 years. If not renewed, one must start from the beginning to once again earn certification.	Referred to as a Profile of Professional Growth, this consists of descriptions about the impact of 3 Professional Growth Experiences and an overall reflection. This must be completed during either certificate years 8–9 or 9–10.

reflection. When you're ready to begin, the "How to Use This Book" section of the Preface offers a guide by candidate type for navigating the most pertinent parts of the book.

Additional Resources

The National Education Association and American Federation of Teachers have partnered to offer resources to teachers pursuing National Board Certification: **http://www.nea.org/home/31738.htm**.

The National Association of State Boards of Education offers a hyperlinked list map of the United States that will take you to any state's board of education. Once on your state's website, search for information about National Board Certification support:

http://nasbe.org/index.php?option=com_contact&view=category&catid= 1119&Itemid=1046.

MY THOUGHTS

(Use this space to record ideas generated from reading this chapter, including the prompts near the end.)

_____

_____

_____

_____

_____

_____

_____

_____

_____

_____

_____

_____

_____

_____

_____

_____

_____

_____

_____

Understanding the Standards

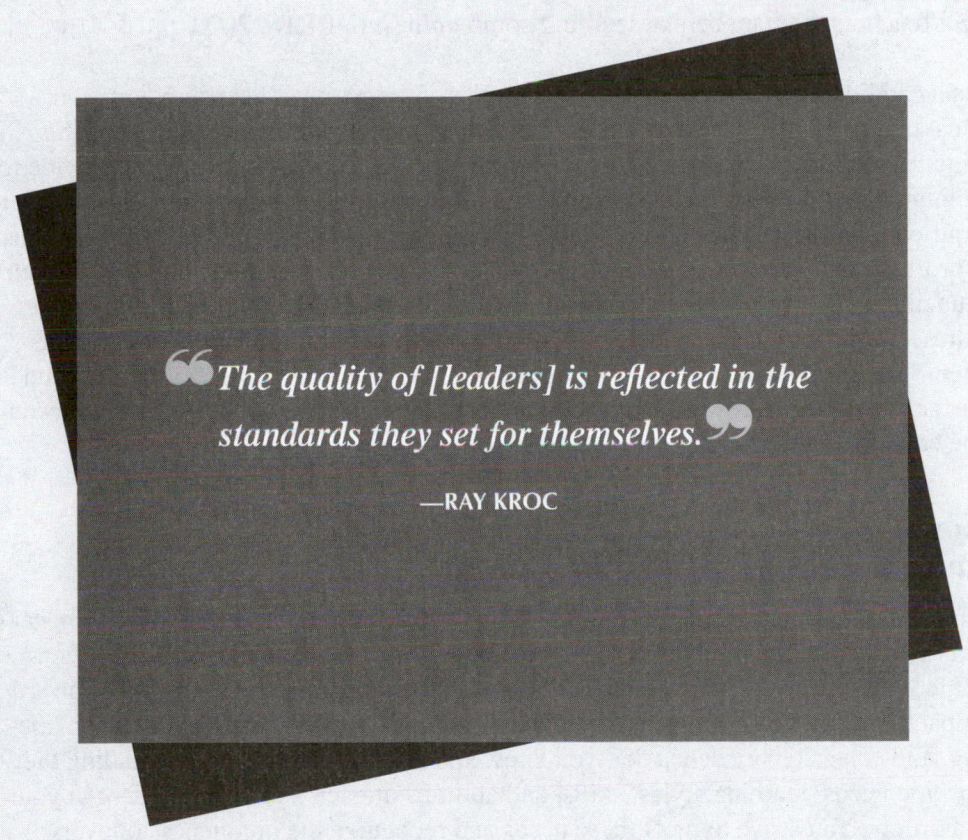

> **"** *The quality of [leaders] is reflected in the standards they set for themselves.* **"**
>
> —RAY KROC

Standards have become a significant force driving what we do in education. As an educator, your everyday work is likely guided to some extent by national, state, and local standards. Sometimes these can be challenging to keep up with, as not all standards are developed with teachers and teaching in mind. Wouldn't it be rewarding to use standards designed solely by and for teachers like yourself to guide and gauge your work as a professional? This is exactly the purpose of the National Board for Professional Teaching Standards (NBPTS), and your work as a National Board candidate will be grounded in the specific standards for your certificate area. It is important to understand these and how they are central to the process of working toward certification.

The Five Core Propositions

The National Board's Five Core Propositions are the foundation upon which each certificate's specific standards are based. These core propositions, as discussed in Chapter 1, are:[1]

1. Teachers are committed to students and their learning.
2. Teachers know the subjects they teach and how to teach those subjects to students.
3. Teachers are responsible for managing and monitoring student learning.
4. Teachers think systematically about their practice and learn from experience.
5. Teachers are members of learning communities. (NBPTS, 2002, pp. 3–4)

As a candidate beginning (or continuing) your journey toward certification, you must determine what each of these propositions means in terms of your teaching practice and think about how they will form the basis of the evidence you provide to demonstrate that you are an accomplished teacher. Stop for a moment and reflect on your own teaching: How does each of the core propositions relate to what you do as a professional? How does it look in your classroom, and what does it mean for your students, to have a learning environment that is created and monitored by a teacher whose philosophy and practice are grounded in these five propositions? The statements and prompts that follow are intended to take your thinking about these even further. Feel free to record your thinking about them in the "My Thoughts" space at the end of the chapter.

Core Proposition 1: Teachers Are Committed to Students and Their Learning

The National Board candidate process stresses the importance of the impact on student learning as the ultimate goal for all teachers. Accomplished teachers are committed to knowing their students well and realize this is the critical first step toward impacting student learning. As a candidate, you will need to provide clear, convincing, and consistent evidence that you know and are dedicated to understanding the specific needs, learning styles, skills, and abilities of each and every student in your classroom. You strive to meet these needs and recognize the uniqueness of every individual student as you provide a successful educational experience for every student. In everything you do, ask yourself: *What do I know about my students, and how does this help me support them as learners and lead to positive learning outcomes?*

Core Proposition 2: Teachers Know the Subjects They Teach and How to Teach Those Subjects to Students

Accomplished teachers know their students first, but they also have a deep understanding of the subjects they teach and how to organize learning experiences that support students in developing the knowledge and skills they need. As a candidate

---

[1]Reprinted with permission from the National Board for Professional Teaching Standards, **www.nbpts. org**. All rights reserved.

you will need to consider how you modify, differentiate, and extend learning to make content meaningful and accessible to all students. What do you know about the required curriculum (and how it builds on prior knowledge and prepares students for what will come later)? How do you supplement the standard curriculum with additional resources and materials to better engage students and further their development and learning? Just as you asked yourself in regard to your knowledge of students, you must ask yourself in everything you do: *What do I know about the subjects I teach, and how does the way in which I teach them impact student learning outcomes?*

Core Proposition 3: Teachers Are Responsible for Managing and Monitoring Student Learning

Through their expertise and knowledge of a wide range of teaching strategies, accomplished teachers create positive and supportive learning environments and monitor student learning regularly through a variety of means. As a candidate, and depending on the requirements of your certificate standards, you will need to articulate how you create such learning environments and provide evidence of how you work with students—as individuals, in various grouping formats, or in whole-class learning situations—to meet their needs. You will need to demonstrate how you monitor student growth and learning, based on goals and objectives, using multiple measures. As you reflect on this proposition, ask yourself: *How do I create an environment that makes learning accessible for all students, and how do I monitor and assess student growth and learning to best impact student outcomes?*

Core Proposition 4: Teachers Think Systematically About Their Practice and Learn From Experience

Accomplished teachers are reflective practitioners who exemplify lifelong learning as they strive to impact each and every student's learning each and every day. As a candidate you will write about your habits of practice and how you analyze both your teaching practices and the outcomes for students as a basis for constantly improving what you do. You will provide evidence of how you have grown and developed as a professional and how this has impacted student outcomes. As you consider what this proposition means in relationship to what you do, ask yourself: *What are the ways in which I think systematically about my practice? How do I use reflection to examine my practice and make modifications that lead to increased student development, learning, and achievement? What am I doing to continue to grow professionally, and how does my growth impact student outcomes?*

> **❝***Even after fourteen years in the classroom, I am a work in progress, but I am always willing to reflect and improve because I want to be the best teacher I can.***❞**
>
> —NBCT, EARLY ADOLESCENCE ENGLISH LANGUAGE ARTS

Core Proposition 5: Teachers Are Members of Learning Communities

High-impact teachers know the importance of learning communities of educators who work together to impact student development and learning. They know that a learning community is multifaceted, and work collaboratively with colleagues, community members, families, and anyone else who might impact student development.

As a candidate you will need to provide evidence of the specific ways in which you reach out to and incorporate the entire learning community in the work you do with your students, and how these efforts have a direct relationship to student outcomes. As you think about your efforts as part of a learning community, ask yourself: *How do I as a member of a learning community reach out, collaborate, and impact student outcomes through these interactions and collaborative efforts?*

Why These Standards?

Why did NBPTS arrive at these core propositions? Recall from Chapter 1 that these standards were developed by a team that consisted of practicing teachers and experts in subject matter content, child development, and higher education. These individuals brought with them significant practical classroom experience as well as knowledge of educational theory and research about effective practice. In addition, significant evidence exists in research literature that these five elements are strongly connected to improved student developmental and learning outcomes. Table 2.1 provides a quick glance at some of the research that supports the ideas of the Five Core Propositions. A more exhaustive look at the research base is provided later in this chapter if you wish to delve deeper.

TABLE 2.1 Research Supporting the Five Core Propositions

Core Proposition	Supporting Research
1. Teachers are committed to students and their learning.	Bransford et al., 2005; Eccles et al., 1993; Eccles & Roeser, 2009; Eccles & Wigfield, 1985; Hamre & Pianta, 2005; Resnick et al.,1997
2. Teachers know the subjects they teach and how to teach those subjects to students.	Ball & Cohen, 1999; Berliner, 2004; Bransford et al., 2005; Scardamalia & Bereiter, 2006; Shulman, 1986
3. Teachers are responsible for managing and monitoring student learning.	Berliner, 2004; Bransford, Brown, & Cocking, 2000; Bransford et al., 2005
4. Teachers think systematically about their practice and learn from experience.	Berliner, 2004; Ertmer & Newby, 1996; Krull et al., 2007; Rodgers, 2002b; Stigler & Hiebert, 1999; Thompson et al., 2009; van Es & Sherin, 2002
5. Teachers are members of learning communities.	Lave & Wenger, 1991; Little et al., 2003; Marzano, 2003; Perkins, 1993; Sheldon, 2003; Sheldon & Epstein, 2005; Tschannan-Moran, 2003

The Cycle of High-Impact Teaching

While the Five Core Propositions are the foundation of the certificate standards, the way in which they are interwoven in a teacher's practice is something that NBPTS refers to as the Architecture of Accomplished Teaching. You will find this structure depicted by NBPTS as a helix and are encouraged to learn about it in materials provided by the organization. From our work with candidates, we have found it helpful to think about this as repeating cycles of setting goals, designing and implementing instruction, assessing student achievement, and reflecting on instruction that represent the actions of a high-impact teacher (see Figure 2.1). We developed this model by extending the ideas offered in the Education Trust's (2005) report, *Gaining Traction, Gaining Ground*, about practices within high-impact high schools. Specifically, a "high-impact" teacher is one whose actions lead to greater than expected learning for his or her students. The visual in Figure 2.1 may be helpful for internalizing and understanding how the core propositions are enacted as well as for identifying and documenting evidence of your impact on students. Note that we use *accomplished* (NBPTS's term) and *high-impact* (our term) interchangeably.

This cycle begins with Core Proposition 1, knowing one's students. While including personal information such as knowing students' likes and dislikes, accomplished teaching goes beyond this. In the context of organizing and planning, the high-impact teacher knows what students already know, how deeply they know it, and what they do not yet know. The high-impact teacher understands the various assets students bring to the classroom (both developmental and cognitive) and how to best help students leverage those attributes to promote further development and learning. All of this takes place against a backdrop of external demands of state standards, local benchmarks, and other curricular requirements. *Goal setting* is the result of a complex set of decisions that includes all these factors.

Once clear goals are identified, the *design and implementation of instruction* (Core Proposition 2) comes next in the cycle. The accomplished teacher knows how best to design engaging and appropriately challenging tasks and activities to help

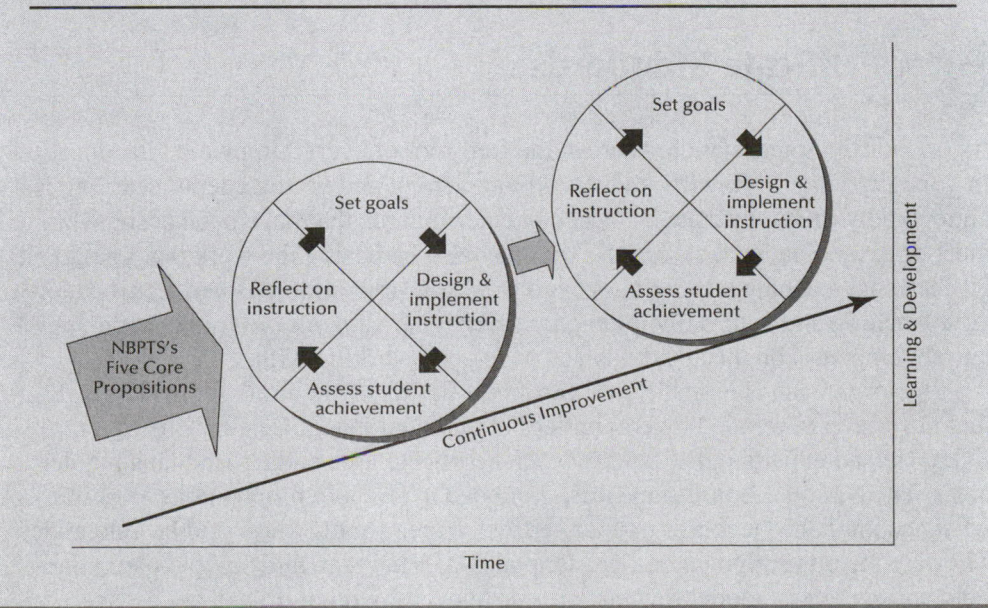

FIGURE 2.1

The Cycle of High-Impact Teaching The cycle of high-impact teaching is a process of goal setting, designing and implementing instruction, assessing student achievement, and reflecting on instruction. Driven by the Five Core Propositions, repeated cycles lead to increases in learning and development over time.

students accomplish specific goals. The cycle continues as the high-impact teacher manages and monitors student learning in response to the instruction and in light of the stated goals (Core Proposition 3). Knowledge of the students, the content, and command of a broad repertoire of skills and techniques for *assessing student achievement* in light of specific goals are characteristic of the high-impact teacher. The constant adjustment and modification of instruction that is at the heart of high-impact teaching is evidenced here.

Core Proposition 4 comes into play as accomplished teachers connect evidence of student outcomes to their teaching decisions, *reflect* on the degree to which goals were met, and think about how to facilitate continued student development and learning. The cycle of goal setting, designing and implementing, assessing, and reflecting can be particularly effective when it includes the input of colleagues, parents, and other stakeholders (Core Proposition 5).

Having completed one such cycle, in light of what was learned the high-impact teacher immediately begins a new cycle with the identification of new goals. It is a continual process of planning, teaching, analyzing, and reflecting. It is important to note that there are often multiple cycles ongoing at any given time—a cycle can occur over the course of a school year, a semester, an instructional unit, or even one day. There can also be multiple "cycles" for multiple students, because not all students have the same learning needs at the same time. Driven by the Five Core Propositions, the Cycle of High-Impact Teaching leads to continuous improvement over time, both in terms of student achievement and one's instructional expertise. The accomplished teacher is a professional who learns from experience and applies this knowledge in future practice. The climb may have its bumps and ruts at times, but generally speaking the accomplished teacher is effective at sustaining progress.

It is important to be aware that in this model, effective reflection occurs *after* some data, whether formal or informal, have been generated and you've taken the opportunity to make sense of what that information means about how well the goals have been met. You'll read more on effective reflection in Chapter 5. At this point, the main idea to remember is that the core propositions are constantly in play, in a disciplined sequence, driving the actions of an accomplished teacher.

The Certificate Standards

As previously noted, standards are at the forefront of everything we do in education. In your everyday work with students, your teaching and your students' learning is undoubtedly driven by state or local content standards that have been designed to meet or exceed national standards. You may also be basing the work that you do on professional teaching standards. As you work toward National Board Certification®, your teaching and your daily interactions with your students will not change your current emphasis on the standards you have been working with.

However, each National Board certificate has its own unique set of standards that have been developed by committees of National Board Certified Teachers (NBCTs) and experts in the field for each certificate area and revised on a regular basis. The National Board standards, grounded in the core propositions, describe what accomplished teachers in your certificate area should know and be able to do. They are meant to supplement, not supplant, all other standards in that particular field and serve as a model for standards developed by other organizations, such as the International Reading Association (IRA), National Council of Teachers of Mathematics (NCTM), National Association for the Education of Young Children (NAEYC), National Council of Teachers of English (NCTE), and National Science Teachers Association (NSTA).

The specific standards for your National Board certificate will be the lens through which you focus as you respond to the questions asked of you in the portfolio entries and assessment center exercises. Through the lens of your specific certificate standards you must be able to describe, analyze, and reflect on your teaching and professional practices and how you are able to impact student development, learning, and achievement. Further, you must be able to document and provide clear, consistent, and convincing evidence that you have met your certificate standards.

A critical first step in working toward National Board Certification is a thorough understanding of your certificate standards. You should begin by reading through the entire certificate standards document, highlighting and making notes of what strikes you as important to remember. As you move through the candidate process, reread the standards over and again, continuing to revise and refine your notes. You will refer to these standards extensively throughout the process and must be intimately familiar with them as you work toward certification. Ultimately, the goal is to see yourself as an accomplished educator whose teaching practices, professional growth, and students' development and learning are driven by these standards.

As mentioned earlier, the certificate standards are built on the foundation of the core propositions. It will be important in your portfolio entries to demonstrate that you recognize this connection. To help you make explicit the relationship between the core propositions, your specific certificate standards, and your professional practices, consider completing a table like the one shown in Table 2.2 for *each* of the propositions (so you end up with five charts when you're finished). This will give you the opportunity to review your certificate standards, think about how they relate to each of the core propositions, and systematically connect them to your professional practices and student outcomes. It is worth taking time to do this exercise early in the process to generate a clear vision of what you're trying to document and describe. An example of how an Early Childhood Generalist candidate might complete this for Core Proposition 1 is shown in Table 2.3. Again, we encourage you to make one table like this for each of the Five Core Propositions using the standards for the certificate area you are pursuing.

> 66 *The certificate standards, combined with state standards for teaching, and teaching standards for teachers gave me a lot to think about. I learned that I can never say I have it all under control, and I know for certain that I need to always reflect and refine. Each student, each year, even each lesson are unique experiences. There's no way I can just do what I have done before and expect to be satisfied with my performance.* 99
>
> —NBCT, EARLY CHILDHOOD GENERALIST

Core Proposition	Related Certificate Standard(s)	The High-Impact Teacher
		What this looks like, feels like, sounds like in my classroom, for my students, and for my professional development.
		What is the impact on student development and learning?

TABLE 2.2 The Five Core Propositions, The National Board Certificate Standards, and the High-Impact Teacher

TABLE 2.3 Example of Core Proposition 1, the National Board Certificate Standards, and the High-Impact Teacher

Core Proposition 1	Related Certificate Standard(s)	The High-Impact Teacher
Teachers are committed to students and their learning.	I Understanding Young Children II Equity, Fairness, and Diversity III Promoting Child Development and Learning IV Knowledge of Integrated Curriculum V Multiple Teaching Strategies for Meaningful Learning	*What this looks like, feels like, sounds like in my classroom, for my students, and for my professional development.* For example, an Early Childhood Generalist candidate responding to this prompt might be thinking about the following: ● Is my classroom more child-centered or teacher-centered? ● Whose voices am I hearing in my classroom, and how does what they are saying provide evidence that learning is taking place? ● What are my expectations for students, and how are these communicated to students? ● What evidence do I have of how well students understand what is expected of them? ● How is instruction tailored or differentiated to meet every child's needs ensuring growth and success? ● In what ways do I facilitate children's learning and ask questions of and elicit responses from children? ● How do I ensure students know and understand the goals and objectives they are working toward? *What is the impact on student development and learning?* ● Children are actively engaged in meaningful, developmentally appropriate learning activities. ● Listening to voices in the classroom reveals that children are doing most of the talking as they engage in questioning, inquiring, discussing, and reflecting on learning. ● Children's work demonstrates an ability to apply higher-level thinking skills and problem solve. ● Children's questions and responses demonstrate deep understanding of specific concepts or skills. ● Students can articulate, orally and in their submitted work, the goals and objectives I have set for them and describe evidence of their progress toward meeting these.

Digging Deeper into the Core Propositions

You may find it helpful to explore the core propositions more deeply. The next section includes brief descriptions of research supporting each of them, followed by bulleted prompts that encourage you to make connections between the propositions, educational research, and evidence of the impact of your teaching practices on student development and learning. Although it is not mandatory to relate your entries to research, it is our belief that as professionals it is often helpful to be able to point to both standards and research to support and further develop our practices.

Core Proposition 1: Teachers Are Committed to Students and Their Learning

Eccles and colleagues' (1993) theory of stage–environment fit states that the degree of alignment between a child's developmental needs (such as autonomy, peer acceptance, and supportive relationships with caring adults) and the environment provided both at home and at school is related to the level of social, academic, and emotional turmoil experienced by youths. When children's needs are well met by their environment, problematic behaviors tend to be avoided. Conversely, when there is a misalignment between student needs and opportunities afforded by the school environment, emotional, social, and academic problems are likely to arise. Eccles and colleagues identify adolescence as a time of particular risk, where changing psychological needs such as increased desire for autonomy, increased peer orientation, and increased cognitive power do not match up well with the traditional parenting and schooling trends of limiting autonomy, limiting collaborative tasks, and failing to provide tasks of greater intellectual complexity during this time.

- What are the developmental needs (physical, emotional, cognitive, language, social) of my students, and what evidence do I have that my actions consistently meet these needs?

- In what ways can I better meet students' needs, and how do I know this?

Eccles and Wigfield (1985) argue that teacher expectations strongly contribute to student achievement. In classrooms with teachers who express high expectations and a belief that students can learn, student achievement is higher than their peers with teachers who do not demonstrate this commitment.

- What evidence do I have that I set and communicate high expectations for my students?

- How does my teaching reflect my belief that all students can and will learn?

- What evidence do I have that students understand what is expected of them?

- How do I ensure that my expectations match my instructional and assessment practices (and what do I do when there is a mismatch)?

Research by Hamre and Pianta (2005) provides strong evidence for the importance of positive teacher–student relationships. A national sample of 910 children who were identified by their kindergarten teachers as having multiple problems (social, academic, behavior, and attention) were divided into two groups: One group was placed with a supportive first-grade teacher; the second group was placed with a less-supportive teacher. By year's end, the at-risk students placed with a teacher who provided high levels of instructional and emotional support scored as well as their peers who were not at risk, while those with a less-supportive teacher continued to struggle. Positive teacher–student relationships continue to be important in middle and high school. In a longitudinal study of over 12,000 students in Grades 7 through 12, Resnick et al. (1997) found that positive relationships with teachers and other measures of "school connectedness" acted as a protective factor against a variety of student health risk factors, such as drug and alcohol use, violent behavior, emotional distress, suicide, and sexual activity.

- How do I consistently provide instructional and emotional support for my students?
- What evidence do I have from students that they feel supported?
- In what ways can I be more supportive of my students, and how do I know this?

Core Proposition 2: Teachers Know the Subjects They Teach and How to Teach Those Subjects to Students

Shulman (1986) introduced the term *pedagogical content knowledge* (referred to as PCK by pedagogy wonks), which he defined as "a blending of content and pedagogy into an understanding of how particular topics, problems, or issues are organized, represented, and adapted to the diverse interests and abilities of learners, and presented for instruction" (p. 8). A teacher's pedagogical content knowledge has subsequently been found to be an indicator of effectiveness by numerous studies (Ball & Cohen, 1999; Berliner, 2004; Bransford, Darling-Hammond, & LePage, 2005).

- What evidence do I have that I know my content well and know how best to teach it?
- How does this knowledge help me determine the best sequence for teaching related ideas?
- How well do I anticipate and address student misconceptions?
- How can I clearly articulate evidence that I consistently use multiple methods or approaches to support student learning, development, and achievement?
- What knowledge do I have that informs this decision making?

Core Proposition 3: Teachers Are Responsible for Managing and Monitoring Student Learning

Berliner (2004), in a study of "expert" teachers, identified the following characteristics: more extensive pedagogical content knowledge; better problem-solving strategies; better adaptation and modification of goals for diverse learners; more ambitious objectives for students; better monitoring of learning and providing feedback; greater display of a passion for teaching. A study of 92 highly effective K–8 teachers in Tennessee revealed a shared set of consistent actions including monitoring student learning by moving throughout the classroom; organizing multiple small-group activities; encouraging student participation in discussion and academic conversations; managing lesson flow from planning activities to arrangement and availability of materials; and displaying student work in the classroom (Bransford et al., 2005). The researchers were also struck by what was *infrequent* in these classrooms: teachers standing at the front lecturing; students working individually with desks in traditional rows; teachers using instructional time ineffectively.

- What evidence do I have of how my teaching consistently exhibits these actions and characteristics?
- What evidence do I routinely collect about my students' development and learning, and how do I use this to modify instruction to better support student development and learning?
- In what ways do I clearly provide feedback to students that supports their continued growth?

Core Proposition 4: Teachers Think Systematically About Their Practice and Learn From Experience

Ertmer and Newby (1996) identified several characteristics of expert learners (which is an essential characteristic of the highly effective teacher): experts are strategic, self-regulated, and reflective. It is not simply the amount of knowledge or skills one possesses, but rather the ability to self-regulate learning that makes him or her expert. Experts know their strengths and weaknesses and adjust their actions accordingly. To evaluate their effectiveness, experts systematically consider their initial goal(s) while examining both the outcomes of their actions and the processes they used.

- In what ways do my actions demonstrate an understanding of the task and draw on my strengths?
- What evidence do I have that I systematically evaluate the effectiveness of my teaching and the lesson(s) used?
- What evidence do I collect about outcomes and processes, and how do I analyze it to inform and improve my teaching?

Van Es and Sherin (2002) have written about teachers learning to "notice" student thinking through collaborative examination of classroom videos and student work samples. They studied a group of elementary teachers over the course of a year as they developed skills in noticing—identifying specific instances in video or aspects of student work that gave insights into students' thinking. As the teachers became more adept at noticing, their written reflections shifted from narrative descriptions of what occurred (first I did this, then I did that) to become more organized around "analytic chunks" (e.g., recognizing a significant incident, relating it to a principle of teaching or learning, processing what the evidence provided says about students' learning, and reflecting on how this informs their own practice as teachers). Through this research van Es and Sherin found that expert teachers are more focused on what *students* do and say, allowing them to better understand student thinking and learning. Similarly, Krull, Oras, and Sisack (2007) found that when given a video of teaching to analyze, expert teachers tended to focus their attention on "teaching and learning as a joint activity" and "learner activities and learning" than novices who primarily focused on "teaching activities."

- What do I "notice" when I look at my teaching artifacts (videos, student work samples, lesson plans, etc.)?
- Do I focus on my actions and words, or those of my students?
- How do I go beyond a narrative description of my teaching to highlight instances of student action or speech that provide insight into their thinking processes?
- When I make evaluations of my teaching (this went well; this did not go well), what evidence are they based on?

Core Proposition 5: Teachers Are Members of Learning Communities

Many researchers espouse the value of working collaboratively as professionals. Perkins (1993) describes the "person-plus" model of learning where the learner draws on surrounding resources (tools, other learners, texts) to construct new under-standing. This is certainly true in teaching. In a study of four schools using vari-ous models for examining student work (Little, Gearhart, Curry, & Kafka, 2003), researchers identified several characteristics associated with effective collabora-tive practice: Participants used tools to structure and focus their investigations and discussion; participants shared pedagogical content knowledge across disciplines (math, English, science, social studies); participants welcomed critical dialogue—they disagreed openly, but respectfully challenged assertions and asked tough ques-tions; and participants were led by a facilitator who maintained a level of comfort and trust while challenging the group to engage in critical dialogue.

- What resources do I draw on to examine artifacts of teaching?
- What additional resources would be useful?
- What is my focus when I examine these artifacts?
- What evidence can I provide demonstrating my willingness to ask "hard ques-tions" about teaching and learning?
- How do my collaborative efforts impact student learning within and beyond my classroom?

Tschannan-Moran (2003) conducted a study of 50 schools in a large urban district. Teachers, principals, parents, and students were surveyed about their own level of collaboration, participation, and trust with each of the other groups. Results revealed that all three factors were strongly related to one another. In particular, a recipro-cal relationship existed between parents and all other groups—the level of trust and collaboration with parents strongly influenced trust and collaboration between other groups. A study by Sheldon (2003) of 82 elementary schools found that in schools that "worked harder to overcome challenges to family and community involvement," students earned higher scores on standardized state achievement tests, establishing a connection between opportunities for meaningful involvement and student develop-ment and learning. A more recent study by Sheldon and Epstein (2005) indicated that the *quality* of parental involvement matters and subject-specific activities that encourage child–family interaction and participation may influence student achieve-ment in the target subject area.

- What do I do to increase the level of trust between myself and various stake-holders (e.g., colleagues, administrators, students, and students' parents and guardians)?
- What do I do to overcome challenges faced by students' families or caregivers to being actively involved with their child's learning?
- What opportunities do I provide for productive involvement of families?

The Next Step

Now that you've had an opportunity to study the National Board standards and core propositions in depth, you are ready to get started with the certification process! Chapter 3 will give you a detailed look at the logistics of the candidate process with specific "to-do" lists for those pursuing *Take One!*, full candidacy, retake candidacy, and renewal. Chapter 4 will get you thinking deeply about the process of reflection, which is at the heart of your work toward certification and will provide guidance on how best to enter into this process.

MY THOUGHTS

Use this space to record ideas generated from reading this chapter, including the prompts about each of the Five Core Propositions.

_____

_____

_____

_____

_____

_____

_____

_____

_____

_____

_____

_____

_____

_____

_____

_____

Getting Started

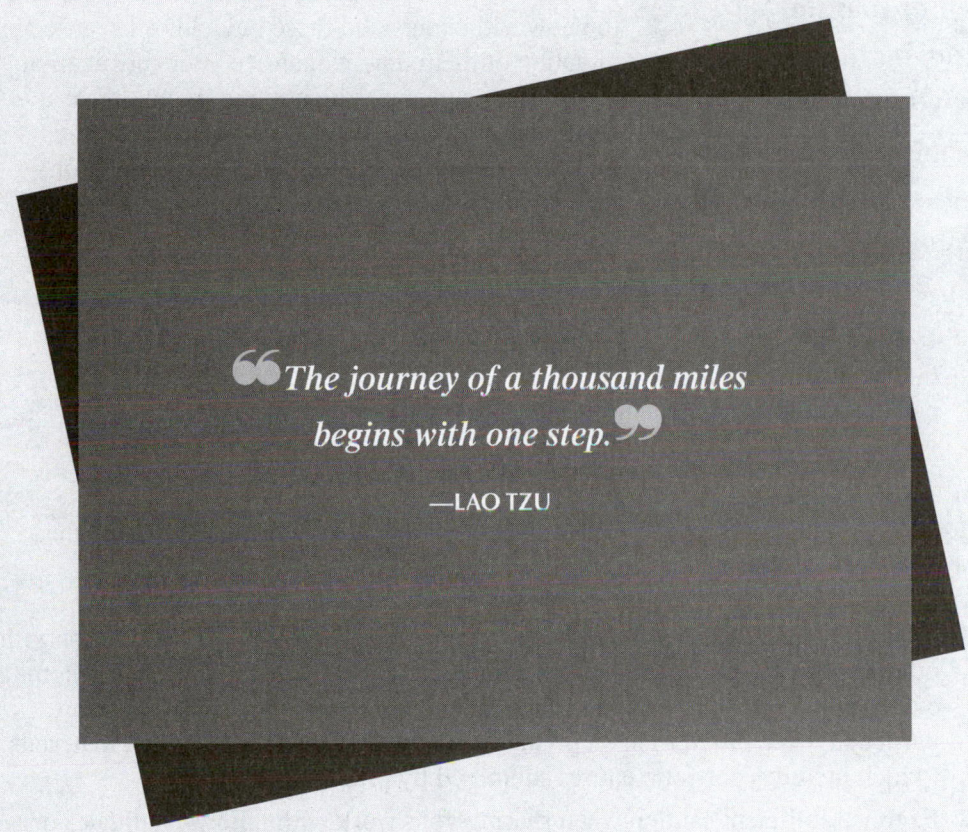

> **"** *The journey of a thousand miles begins with one step.* **"**
>
> —LAO TZU

The National Board Certification process is both challenging and greatly satisfying. The rewards are profound, personally and professionally. Time and again, teachers report the process as transformative to their practice. With a little organizational support, completing the National Board Certification process can be a hugely positive professional growth experience. We will give you some pointers in this chapter to help you get off on the right foot as you start your journey that will, if not involve a thousand miles, certainly involve thousands of words.

Ethical Guidelines for Candidates

We know that as an education professional you come to your work with a strong sense of ethics—after all, you're trusted with other people's children. Since National Board Certification® is a high-stakes examination of your professional practice, it is important to take into consideration some matters related to how this work is done from an ethical standpoint. To ensure the validity, professional value, and integrity of the assessment, the National Board for Professional Teaching Standards (NBPTS) has established ethical guidelines for candidates, support providers, assessors, and institutions of higher education that may use the National Board portfolio as part of a degree program. It is important to know and understand these guidelines because any violation of them may jeopardize your certification or ability to pursue certification in the future. You might think some of these are obvious, but others will perhaps give pause for careful consideration. Specifically, NBPTS policies state that candidates cannot:

> 66*I was so excited when I received my box, but once I opened it up and started looking at all the material on the CD, I was overwhelmed. I didn't even know where to start. I thought, "What have I gotten myself into?"*99
>
> —NBCT, ADOLESCENCE AND YOUNG ADULTHOOD SCIENCE

(1) Falsify or fabricate evidence for any entries; (2) copy the work of other teachers or NBCTs to use in their own portfolios; (3) give, ask for, or receive information on secure assessment materials or information; or (4) share, publish, electronically post or otherwise reproduce secure assessment materials or information. (NBPTS, 2008, p. 2)

To protect yourself and your work, we advise that you consider taking the following precautions:

1. Exercise reasonable care when deciding to work with a support provider or with other candidates going through the process. Do what you can to ensure whomever you work with is well informed about guidelines for candidate support, particularly the prohibition on giving or receiving "secure assessment materials" (which includes portfolio entries submitted by prior candidates).

2. Exercise sufficient caution when sharing your work with fellow candidates or support providers. For example, if working with a cohort of candidates when bringing several hard copies of an entry for feedback during a support session, make it your responsibility to collect these back at the end of the session. If electronic communication is a part of your candidate support, ensure such transmissions are secure and consider sending only parts of an entry (rather than your entire entry) to minimize the risk of your work being utilized by another candidate. While you may be justified in trusting a colleague with whom you are going through the assessment process, electronic communications in particular can get into the wrong hands through unintended actions (e.g., spyware and viruses).

3. Do not expect or allow a support provider to tell you that your work will or will not "pass" or prescribe for you what evidence to collect or lesson to video record. Such evaluative input is not in the spirit of the National Board

Certification process and is not permitted per the ethical support guidelines for NBPTS-trained candidate support providers. A support provider *should* ask critical questions to elevate your thinking and help you reflect on how you are providing evidence of meeting your certificate standards, but *should not* be judgmental or make important decisions for you.

4. Do not expect or allow a support provider to attempt scoring your work by telling you "This is a four" or "This will certify." Only trained teams of assessors can make such determinations. Candidate support is about helping you examine your work through the lens of the National Board standards, not about scoring your work.

5. Know that once entries and videos are submitted to NBPTS they become confidential assessment documents owned by the organization. For this reason, submitted entries cease to be the property of the candidate and *cannot* be shared with others. Doing so will violate the terms of assessment to which you agreed when registering as a candidate and could lead to a cancellation of your scores and revocation of your certification.

Starting Your Journey

Once you have decided to pursue National Board Certification, *Take One!,* or renewal, there is no need to wait until you receive your box of assessment instructions and materials from the National Board—get started now! We've listed some first steps and tips to help you get you going in the right direction.

First Steps for All Candidates

There are several important pieces to put into place in order to start your transformational journey through the National Board process off on the right foot.

1. Pay fees to NBPTS to be issued a candidate ID number and establish a username and password to access the NBPTS My Profile site to manage your candidate account. *Note:* When completing your online application, be sure to select the option that states you wish to be considered for candidate scholarships or grants from third parties. This way, NBPTS will automatically consider you for any of these for which you are eligible.

2. Complete any required forms as outlined in your portfolio instructions.

3. Verify that you are an active candidate by attempting to log in to your NBPTS My Profile candidate account. You should log in regularly to check for any notices, updates, and deadlines regarding your candidacy. You can monitor the status of your fees and forms here as well.

4. If you have not already done so, find out what support your district, state, or region may provide for National Board candidates. Some may cover fees, allow for release days, provide a stipend upon completion, or offer support for videotaping, copying materials, postage costs, and so on.

5. Go to **www.nbpts.org** to locate National Board Certified Teachers (NBCTs) in your certificate area who may be potential sources of support. Whereas a candidate support provider may be from your local area, with the Internet

it is possible to support candidates from a distance. Is there a recognized NBCT network in your area? Are there formal programs to support candidates?

6. Some colleges and universities organize support for candidates. Check with local campuses to find out if this is available nearby. If you are told that the portfolio can be used to satisfy requirements for a master's degree or other credit-earning courses, ask if the institution has a signed agreement with the National Board to use candidate work in this manner, since technically, once submitted, your portfolio entries are considered confidential assessment documents and become property of NBPTS.

Organizational Tips for All Candidates

Once you've taken care of the logistics above it's time to get organized. This will ensure you make the most of the time you'll invest in this process.

1. Locate and download the portfolio instructions, the standards, the scoring guides, the evaluation of evidence guide for your certificate area, and other informational materials. These can be found on the CD sent to you from NBPTS or on the NBPTS website. We strongly recommend that you invest in the paper and ink necessary to print these and give yourself access to the full documents in hard-copy format. Figure out a method of organizing them that will help you find needed information—you will be referring to these continually over the course of the assessment process.

2. Develop a systematic method to organize your work and your time. This should include a place to keep student work samples, copies of videos, entry drafts with feedback notes, study notes for the assessment center (if required), and so on.

3. For each entry (or "component" for renewal candidates), use the Entry Planning Worksheet (Table 3.1) to assist you as you complete the following tasks:

   • Read and make note of the format specifications. What type of lesson does each entry require? Do you need to include a video? Do students have to work in small groups? Is the use of technology required? Must student work be collected, and if so, from how many students?

   • Read and become familiar with the specific standards that are to be addressed.

   • Read and become familiar with the scoring guide and evaluation of evidence guide for your certificate area (or for the Profile of Professional Growth if you're a renewal candidate). What types of evidence will you have to document? What will assessors look for in your entry?

We have provided quick tips—specific suggestions developed from our work as candidates ourselves and as support providers with candidates—that are organized by candidate type: full candidates (Table 3.2), retake candidates (Table 3.3), and renewal candidates (Table 3.4). Note that there are no quick tips for *Take One!* candidates because everything they need to know is within the main text of this chapter. The remainder of this chapter focuses on entry planning, something all candidates will benefit from learning about.

TABLE 3.1 Entry Planning Worksheet

Entry Number and Title_____

Notes about specific format specifications (e.g., Video? Length? Groups? Student work? Number of students? Special skills or tools?)

Certificate Standards Assessed	Key Phrases from Scoring Guide that Assess Each Standard	Potential Lessons that Meet Format Specification and Align with Certificate Standards	Approximate Date(s) of Lesson(s)

TABLE 3.2 Full Candidate Quick Tips

Full Candidate Quick Tips

Compare entry specifications to your instructional calendar. Know which of your portfolio entries are based upon work in different instructional units, or over a specific course of time. For such entries, identify *several* potential instructional sequences you might select from and use to generate evidence. In this way you will have some choice when selecting which to include in your portfolio.	Read and note the categories of documented accomplishments required in entry four. Compile a list of possible accomplishments in each category and what type of supporting evidence you would want to collect. Start asking for notes, letters, or verification forms from those who can verify your accomplishments. The Documented Accomplishments Categories Chart in the NBPTS portfolio instructions for entry four may be helpful in organizing your work.	Start keeping a communication log of all contact with parents, colleagues, and community members/organizations if you do not already do so. The portfolio instructions for entry four provide a blank communication log and a sample of what one could look like. These may be helpful in organizing your work.	Although we recommend keeping your primary focus on the portfolio entries early in the process, it is a good idea to have a file in which you can place resources related to the assessment center exercises as you come across them.

TABLE 3.3 Retake Candidate Quick Tips

Retake Candidate Quick Tips

If you have previously worked with a candidate support provider, consider contacting him or her to talk about your plans. If you did not work with a support provider, consider doing so. You might also go to www.nbpts.org to locate NBCTs in your certificate area who may be a potential resource.	Examine your score report and identify which entries you wish to bank (i.e., keep the score) and which you plan to retake. Consider how many points you need to reach 275. How much can you realistically expect to gain from each retake entry? You must pay for each entry, so if cost is a concern you do not want to retake more than you need. On the other hand, if you underestimate you may not be able to pick up sufficient points. Also consider the *relative weighting* of each entry; entry four is weighted the least of the portfolio entries and each of the assessment center exercises are weighted less than any of the portfolio entries. Finally, remember that you may *not* retake any entry on which you earned a 2.75 or better.	You must officially apply to retake. Begin taking steps to continue the journey as soon as possible since the timeline to register as a retake candidate and complete retakes is shorter than for the new candidate. What are the costs involved and when is the deadline to apply for retake candidacy and pay the fees?	Read thoroughly the "What Is Retake Candidacy?" section of Chapter 8.

TABLE 3.4 Renewal Candidate Quick Tips

Renewal Candidate Quick Tips			
Verify that you meet the requirements of having a valid teaching license and are currently in year eight or nine of your National Board certificate. You do *not* need to be a full-time classroom teacher to renew your certification but must have access to students in the same subject area and age range as your certificate.	Having read the requirements and scoring rubric for the three Profile of Professional Growth components, brainstorm potential Professional Growth Experiences and the types of evidence you would need to collect for each. Remember, each must be ongoing, varied, and multifaceted, and impact student learning (either directly or indirectly through work with professional colleagues).	Compare these specifications to your professional calendar and develop a plan for when and how you will collect the required evidence. In particular, for the video in component 2, identify two potential instructional sequences and times you could video record so you will have some choice when selecting which to write about.	Read thoroughly the "Renewing your Certification" section of Chapter 9.

Entry Planning

Because each entry in the National Board is designed for teachers to examine and document different aspects of their work, it is essential that candidates carefully read the format specifications, the certificate standards being addressed, and the scoring criteria. Many excellent teachers doing wonderful, effective work with students fall short of earning National Board Certification because they did not address the required criteria for each entry and did not provide clear, consistent, and convincing evidence of their impact on student development and learning through the lens of their certificate standards.

Overall Planning Considerations

It is best to use backward planning strategies, something you might be familiar with from curriculum planning work, to prepare in advance for how you will generate the evidence necessary to meet the certificate standards. Examine the requirements and think about what instructional sequences you have scheduled this year will best exemplify these. Identify these early and make note of them on your instructional calendar. Try to identify several potential sources of evidence for each entry so you have some flexibility in selecting what you want to focus on for your portfolio entries. *Remember, for full candidates each entry must include a lesson from a different instructional sequence.*

Perhaps you do not think you have an instructional sequence that meets all the needed criteria for a particular entry. Keep in mind there is no perfect lesson. Each classroom and context is different; what works well for one teacher and his or her students at a certain point in time may not work well for a different teacher with a different group of students at a different point in the year. An expert teacher knows what is most effective for his or her students at any given point in time and should be able to describe, analyze, and reflect on his or her instructional choices and impact on student development and learning.

Also know that the National Board does not advocate inventing a lesson or activity solely to attain National Board Certification. Instead, consider this an opportunity to more closely examine your current lessons and teaching practices. How might adding a technology component to an instructional sequence make it more engaging and effective? How would incorporating the use of a manipulative or visual model into an existing small-group exploration better meet students' learning needs? If you have something that works well to support and promote student learning, then do not alter it solely to fit the requirements of a particular entry. Instead, consider whether another, different learning sequence might better demonstrate how your practice addresses the standards for that particular entry. The bottom line—if making changes is likely to improve the lesson's impact on student learning, then consider modifying the lesson. The transformative aspect of the National Board Certification process comes from how the deep analysis and reflection required leads to changes in how teachers approach planning, implementing, and assessing instruction that ultimately have positive impacts on student development, learning, and achievement. The critical consideration in all entries is how a teacher's instructional choices and accomplishments impact student development and learning.

Planning for Video-Based Entries

The video entries in particular involve both logistical and strategic planning. Setting up and operating the recording equipment can be logistically challenging, and it is important you reach out to those with experience using such equipment. In addition, students may behave differently when the camera is present—some shut down and some act out. One strategy to curtail this behavioral issue is to tape lessons you know you will not use as practice lessons. Try setting up the camera in a corner of the classroom, recording a few minutes of class, and allowing students to view the recording. This will both provide both an opportunity to test your equipment (are the camera angles and volume appropriate?) and allow students (and you) to become comfortable with being taped and adjust to the camera (and have some of the novelty wear off).

Here are some considerations when planning for video recording:

- Collect student consent forms (and consents for any adults who will be in the room) before doing any recording.

  - For those without consent, the best solution is to adapt seating arrangements so their faces do not appear on the video. If you'd rather make arrangements for those students to leave the classroom during the videotaping to ensure there are no mishaps, make plans to ensure they will be engaged in productive learning activities aligned to lesson objectives.

- Secure a camera and other needed materials such as microphones and tripods well before you need them so you have time to test them.

> 66*Don't be afraid if your videos don't come out the way you want. Take several videos and find the one that best shows things you did well and things that were unexpected. Sometimes the videos that are 'just in case' turn out better than the one you intended to … use.*99
>
> —NBCT, EARLY CHILDHOOD GENERALIST

- Ideally, arrange for someone to come in and operate the video camera.
- If you are having someone videotape for you, be sure to instruct them on what they can and cannot do and what specifically to focus on or capture in the taping.
- Allow yourself sufficient time to view the recording and select appropriate segments.
- Follow each entry's guidelines on how you are permitted to select and (in some cases) edit the video segment.
- Learn how to convert your video segment to a format accepted by NBPTS (or find someone else with the expertise to do so).
- Allow sufficient time to transcribe and analyze the interactions and dialogue in the video segment.

Although it is important to invest time and energy in collecting good-quality video for these entries, it is equally important to keep in mind that under present NBPTS scoring practices: (a) the video itself is only one part of the entry, (b) the video itself is a piece of evidence that is *not* scored, and (c) the video is viewed only *after* the assessor reads your written commentary. Accordingly, do not get overwhelmed with producing the "perfect" video—it is not as critical as the written commentary you create to accompany it.

Planning for Student Work–Based Entries

The careful selection of student work samples to include with your entries is essential. Be sure to read the requirements of the entry and identify specifically what the assessors will be looking for in the student work. Plan ahead and collect work from all students, even those you might not anticipate including, so that you can make good choices that best demonstrate evidence of the impact your teaching has on student development and learning. Keep in mind that for certain entries you may need work samples that show growth over time. For this purpose, your "best student" may start out performing at a high level and stay there; this may not give you as much to write about compared to the work of a student who started the learning sequence less well prepared but made significant progress. Choose students who will allow you to highlight how well you:

- Understand individual student backgrounds and how they influence instruction and learning.
- Identify each student's strengths and areas for growth based on submitted work.
- Modify instruction to enhance the impact on student development and learning.

Just as with video, it is better to have several choices when preparing for this entry, so collect everything. This potentially will be a lot of paper, so it is also important to develop a method for keeping things organized. For example, save student work with any instructions or rubrics as well as lesson plans so you can remember what instruction came before and after. This will help you demonstrate your role impacting student learning and meeting the needs of the students with whom you work. What this means for you as a candidate is that you will need to demonstrate evidence of how you impact students' growth as a learner. Evidence of growth can and should include a range of indicators; the important thing to consider is how you demonstrate the relationship between your practices and the evidence you provide of the impact on student development and learning. Being able to describe what you planned to do, what actually happened, why it happened, and what impact this had on students is critical.

Planning for the Documented Accomplishments Entry

Entry 4 is different from the others because it focuses on what the teacher does beyond the scope of everyday classroom learning activities. The candidate may select up to a maximum of eight accomplishments to document and analyze. These accomplishments must address the certificate standards, and each should fit into one of three categories (although accomplishments may overlap categories):

- Your work with families and the community of your students within the past year
- Your development as a teacher-learner during the past five years
- Your work as an educational leader or a collaborator during the past five years

The key to selecting accomplishments is to know that you must document the significance and impact (immediate or long-term) of each accomplishment on student development and learning, whether for students in your own classroom or students beyond your classroom or learning environment. Note that this impact may be inferred (e.g., how it is likely to impact future learning for students). So although the accomplishments document activity outside the classroom, a link must explicitly be made to its impact on student development and learning.

It might be helpful to start brainstorming a list of accomplishments that fit each of the three categories. Some accomplishments may fit more than one category. Although assessors are trained to find evidence as they find it, we advise that in the written commentary you make it clear how the activity fits each category. After a list has been generated, start thinking about the impact of each accomplishment and the possible evidence you could collect to document its impact on students. The Documented Accomplishments Categories Chart in the portfolio instructions for Entry 4 may also be helpful in organizing your work.

What's Next?

Now that you've got some ideas for starting your journey on the right foot, it is time to start thinking, dialoguing, and writing about your high-impact teaching. Chapter 4 will describe some best practices for engaging in these processes. From the standpoint of the intellectual work you will do as a candidate, this next chapter is critical for you to thoroughly read, understand, and put into practice as you put together your entries.

(Use this space to record ideas generated from reading this chapter.)

_____

_____

_____

_____

_____

_____

_____

_____

_____

_____

_____

_____

_____

_____

_____

_____

4

Thinking, Dialoguing, and Writing About Teaching

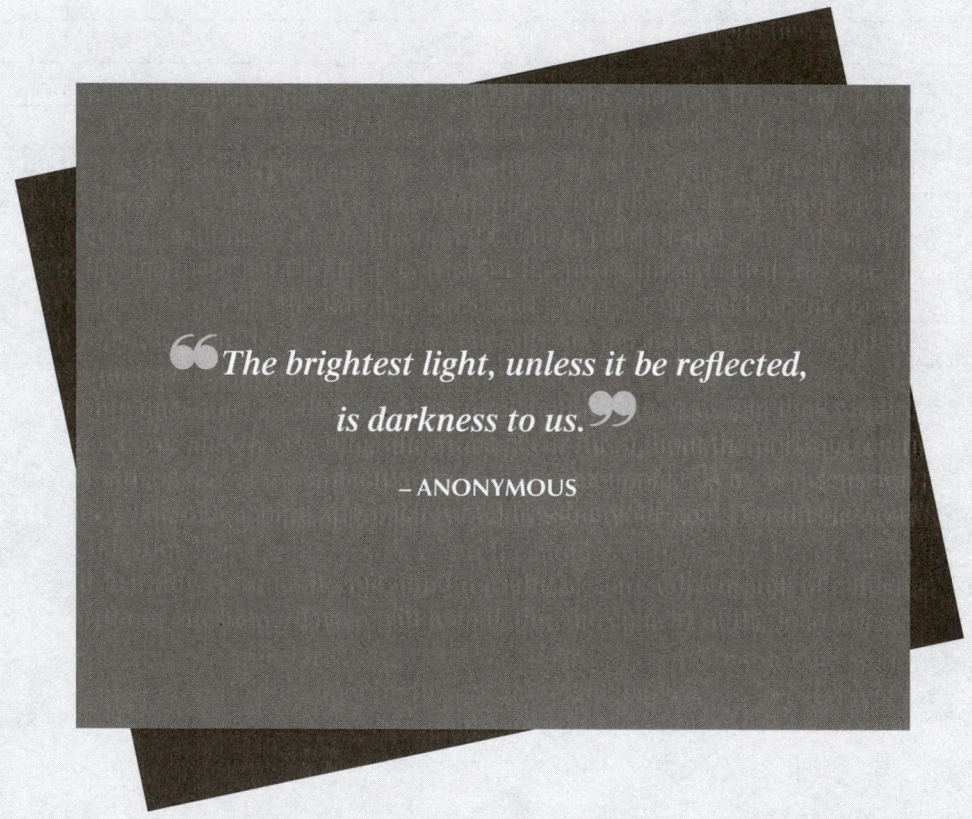

"*The brightest light, unless it be reflected, is darkness to us.*"

– ANONYMOUS

Metacognition, the skill of thinking about your thinking, involves the ability to reflect on experience and use what is learned to inform future action. This is a central component of the Five Core Propositions and an essential part of the portfolio entry writing process. Reflection can be even more powerful when done in peer groups; two (or more) heads may truly be better than one. Indeed, focused discussions about effective teaching practices can be energizing and highly productive under the right conditions. It is critical to know how to structure these professional conversations in order to get the most out of them. Just as important as reflection on your teaching practices is the process of communicating evidence of what you have learned from this and how it informs your future actions and continued growth. The topics of reflection (individual and collaborative) and written communication as they relate to the portfolio process will be addressed in this chapter.

As teachers, we realize it is unrealistic to expect that each lesson will be successful the first time we teach it. However, the mark of a highly effective teacher is the willingness to critically examine each lesson as it was planned and enacted, to collect and evaluate evidence of its impact on student learning in light of the stated goals of the lesson, and to come to some understanding about what might make the lesson better the next time it is taught. Albert Einstein is credited with saying that the definition of insanity is doing the same thing over and over and expecting different results. It is the continuous and habitual process of reflection and revision that sets apart the highly skilled, high-impact teacher.

Like the development of any skill, such as shooting free throws in basketball or sewing a quilt, becoming proficient in reflection requires practice. The good news is, then, reflection is a learned behavior and can improve over time. Numerous studies show that novice teachers tend not to be as adept at reflecting in action since the general demands of teaching monopolize too much active attention for them to be able to teach, reflect, and adjust all at the same time. On the other hand, accomplished teachers have become proficient with reflecting in the moment and immediately adjusting instruction as needed during the lesson in progress. The challenge for you as a National Board candidate, no matter your level of experience as a teacher, is to learn to unpack this "reflection in action" to identify and describe in writing the myriad decisions you make during a lesson. In effect, you will need to take time to explicitly recognize your habits of reflection and revision.

John Dewey distinguished reflection as a skill different and more rigorous than other forms of thought. It requires a specific mind-set: The reflective teacher is enthusiastic and curious about his or her practice, self-confident in his or her ability as a professional, yet willing to act when shortcomings are identified and able to consider new ideas and alternative viewpoints.

Take a moment to consider your responses to the following questions (and consider jotting them down in the "My Thoughts" space at the end of the chapter). This will help you begin to make "public" your private actions of reflection and revision as an entry point into the process of crafting your National Board candidate portfolio.

- In what ways do I demonstrate *enthusiasm* for teaching, learning, and my content?
- How do my actions as an educator demonstrate that I have *confidence* in my professional experience and skills?
- What forms of evidence do I use to know whether learning is occurring, and how do I *act on the findings* to make adjustments to improve my practice?
- What are some of the ways I *invite and seek out new ideas and feedback* from peers about my teaching practice?

The Four Phases of Reflection

Reflection is a rigorous and disciplined process of thinking that involves a progression through four phases:

1. Framing and focusing evidence
2. Noticing and identifying evidence

3. Analyzing evidence

4. Acting on evidence

Let's briefly examine each of these phases.

Framing and Focusing Evidence

The *framing and focusing* phase requires you to be clear about the purpose(s) or goal(s) of the lesson or instructional sequence you are examining. The following set of questions will help you articulate the outcomes you have in mind for a particular lesson or instructional sequence.

- What, specifically, are students supposed to know or be able to do after the completion of the lesson?
- What would evidence of this learning look like?
- What opportunities were created—planned or in the moment decisions—to help students learn?
- Why were those choices made (as opposed to other choices)?

Noticing and Identifying Evidence

Once these questions are answered, the phase of *noticing and identifying evidence* can begin.

- What, specifically, do you notice or home in on about what students do or say that provides evidence of their development or learning?
- How can you identify evidence of how well students achieved the goals you had set?

Analyzing Evidence

Following the collection of evidence, the next phase is *analysis*.

> **"***Doing a lesson study [reflection] is like putting up an x-ray to your teaching process. It is intense. It shows you parts of your teaching you never knew were there or gives you a clearer view of what you only slightly knew was there.***"**
>
> —NBCT, ADOLESCENCE AND YOUNG ADULTHOOD ART

- What does that evidence tell you about what students now know or are able to do?
- What was not learned so well?
- Who learned and who did not? What do students know and how deeply do they understand or know it?

Acting on Evidence

Finally, the *acting on evidence* phase requires you to connect the analysis to actual teaching practices in order to take action.

- How did your instruction contribute, or fail to contribute, to students' development, learning, and achievement?
- How might a change in instruction result in improved outcomes?
- What changes need to be implemented?
- How and why would those changes improve the lesson?

Each portfolio entry requires that you go through each of these phases of the reflection process. Carefully read each entry's prompts and answer all the questions. The National Board does not intend that this process be a secret. During the scoring of your entries, assessors are trained to use the frame and focus *you provide* to validate the evidence *you provide*, understand the analysis *you provide* of that evidence, and determine if the conclusions *you provide* are reasonable. The point? It is how well *you provide* this information that is critical. Look at the portfolio as your opportunity to get on paper and provide a lens for the National Board process to demonstrate what you think about your lesson or learning sequence before, during, and after its implementation. The portfolio is simply an external public record of the internal private dialogue taking place as you reflect on your work. You may find the Evidence Analysis Guide (Figure 4.1) helpful as a tool to organize and record your thinking and writing. This tool is informed by the work of Hiebert, Morris, Berk, and Jansen (2007) and Santagata, Zannoni, and Stigler (2007).

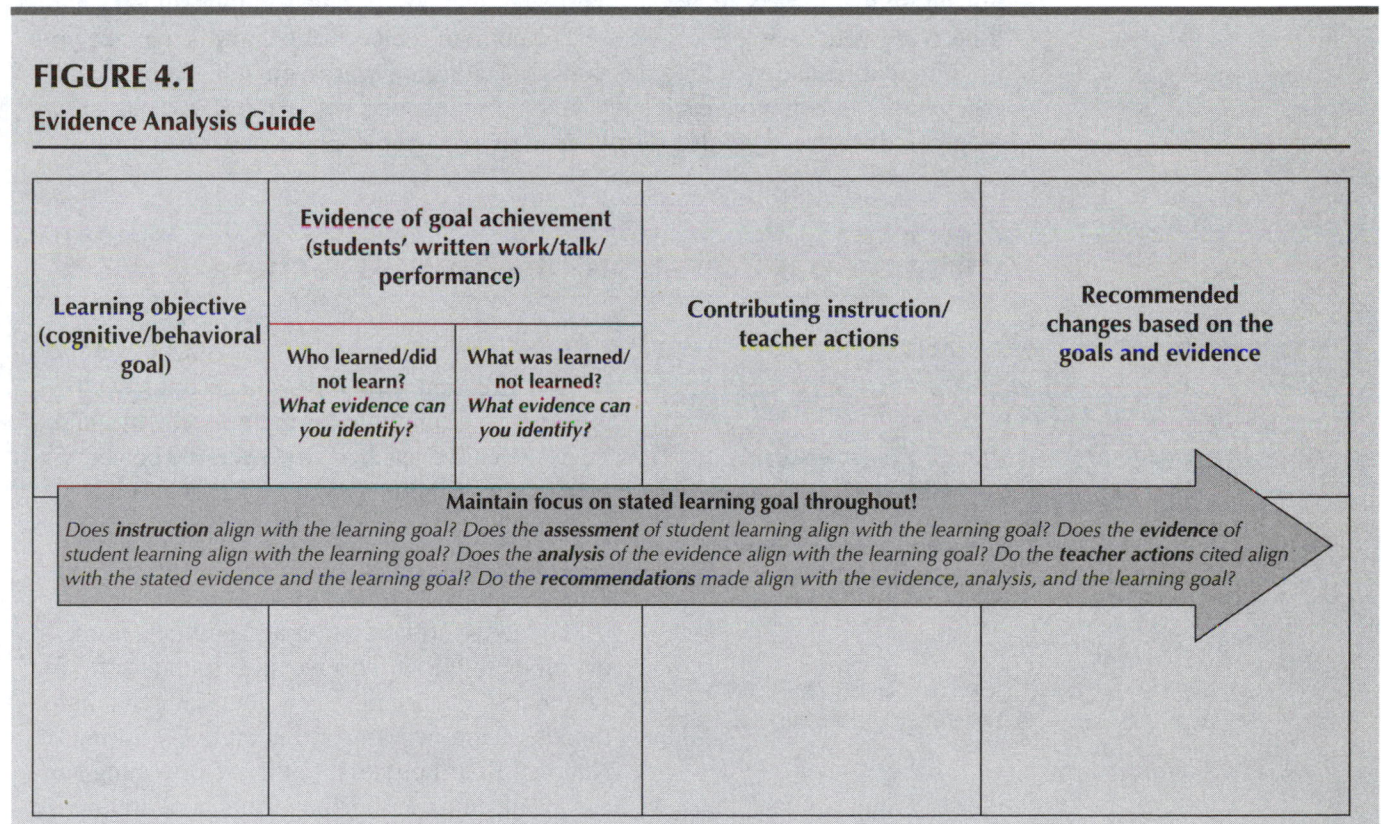

FIGURE 4.1

Evidence Analysis Guide

Providing the Whole Picture

From our experiences working with candidates, we have learned that one of the most important aspects of putting together a strong entry is for you to keep a focus on how the four phases of reflection are part of the larger whole. Having described well the goals for a learning sequence does not preclude the need for you to provide further description and analysis of the instructional activities implemented, a discussion of the evidence that students met the goals, and reflection on what worked well and what might be modified for next time. Similarly, an outstanding learning activity alone is not sufficient to demonstrate expert practice—it is how you connected the activity to predetermined goals and to student learning outcomes that make the case. Finally, it is not enough that you write about lesson modifications as an example of being reflective; the modifications must be based on clear, specific evidence that came from the learning sequence and are connected to its goals.

For example, consider this statement: "It is evident from the discussion between the student in red and the student in black that they understood." Left unanswered is what specifically about the discussion served as evidence that students had achieved a specific learning goal and what about the instruction provided supported this result. Be specific in your evidence when making your case— think about the whole picture.

Finally, be sure to explicitly acknowledge, and take credit for, your instructional decisions. If you have students in groups of three, explain why (and why not groups of four, or two?). If you have students read *The Giver* by Lois Lowry, explain why you chose that text. Why was that particular text appropriate for your students at that time given your instructional goals? The point of the portfolio entry is to make your thinking public and visible to the assessors. Constantly ask yourself, "Why?" and "So what?" as you write each entry. If you can respond with a more in-depth answer, then you likely have not dug deeply enough into your teaching and reflection.

Professional Conversations About Teaching

> 66 *I credit my being certified on my first try to the fact that I was able to collaborate with other candidates in the process. It was the most valuable professional development I have been a part of in my 29 years of teaching.* 99
>
> —NBCT, EARLY AND MIDDLE CHILDHOOD READING–
> LANGUAGE ARTS/EARLY AND MIDDLE CHILDHOOD

Reflection can be a wholly independent exercise done in isolation. Certainly you do not have to be part of a group in order to be a reflective and highly effective teacher. However, the power of productive collaboration to spur professional growth is at the heart of Core Proposition 5: Teachers are members of learning communities. This section will contribute to your knowledge of productive collaboration and outline a process of collaborative support we have found useful for candidates. This section is written for candidates thinking about working collaboratively during the National Board process. For those providing support to groups of candidates we have an appendix at the end of this book to provide guidance about such a role.

A *learning community* of educators is a group of peers who share the values and goals necessary to improve educational practice by engaging in critical dialogue about teaching that includes honest, evidence-based examinations and discussions of the effectiveness of their actions (Lave and Wenger, 1991; Lord, 1994; National Research Council, 2000). These professional discussions are structured investigations of artifacts of educational activities (such as videos, student work, and assessment results) during which the group examines evidence of not only what students learned and how well they learned it, but also what students did not learn and why they failed to learn it.

As you can imagine, this sort of professional conversation requires a significant amount of trust, self-confidence, patience, and humility among the members. Although all teachers take pride in their actions as educators, in order for the learning community to function well it is important to distance yourself somewhat from the evidence being discussed. Establishing a formal protocol to structure such discussions helps remind members that it is the *process* that is important, not the individual teacher. In other words, whereas reflection is a personal act, the learning community's discussion of specific evidence and artifacts should be less personal—it is about the students, it is about their work, it is about their learning. Members of a learning community should approach the task with the mind-set of improving practice. It is through critical examination and questioning—challenging unstated assumptions and making note of critical details—that growth occurs. What follows are some tips that your learning community may find helpful in establishing and maintaining a respectful and productive tone.

Guidelines for Professional Dialogue

These guidelines are an amalgamation of our professional experience and a variety of published sources, including *The Adaptive School* by Garmston and Wellman (1999); *Crucial Conversations* by Patterson, Grenny, McMillan, and Switzler (2002); *Flawless Consulting* by Block (1981); *The Handbook of Coaching* by Hudson (1999); and *Being an Effective Mentor* by Jonson (2002). All are excellent resources and are included in the reference list at the end of this book.

1. **Use a protocol.** Protocols help focus the discussion and maintain a professional tone. The Looking at Student Work Collaborative website (**www.lasw. org**) offers several models. Take a look at these and have your learning community choose one or two to test out, with the goal of eventually settling on one that everyone is comfortable with.

2. **Ask questions rather than dispense advice.** Honor each candidate's journey. It is up to each member of your learning community to collectively help one another recognize discrepancies or concerns, but each member should decide individually how to address these in her or his own practice. Everyone must arrive at their own solution in their own time. The well-functioning learning community will ask critical questions that lead to more effective personal reflection.

3. **Describe rather than evaluate.** When discussing what you notice or see, describe your observations and avoid making evaluative statements. For example, "I notice the student body language in this group—they lean forward and point at the work," versus "The engaged body language of the students in this group is great."

4. **Establish a "third point."** When discussing evidence, place it on the table (or in the case of video, in the video player). This literal "distancing" helps depersonalize it as it becomes a neutral third point of discussion. Discussion becomes about the evidence, not about any one member.

5. **Speak for yourself.** Avoid using *we* when you mean *I*.

6. **Get to the point.** When asking questions, be specific and keep it brief.

7. **Give it with care.** Be critical and honest, but not mean-spirited.

8. **Assume positive presuppositions.** When responding to probing questions from colleagues, remind yourself that your colleagues are asking the questions to help you, and every member of your learning community, learn and grow, not to tear you down. Those who care about you and your craft will be willing to push.

9. **Be proactive.** If some action is hampering the effectiveness of your learning community, address this right away! For example, "When you are late, it makes it difficult to get the most out of our limited time together."

If it takes so much organization and effort to do well, is working collaboratively really worth it? Absolutely! Working with a group will allow you to contribute positively to the growth of colleagues as well as yourself, which is invigorating. You also get the benefit of different perspectives, unbiased views of your teaching, and expertise in areas other than your own. Finally, knowing you are accountable to others to have made progress on your portfolio when you meet helps provide that extra push you sometimes may need to stay on track for completion. Quite simply, being part of a well-functioning learning community of candidates is one of the best experiences of the process.

A Question Well Put Is Half-Answered

> **❝**Collaboration also meant accountability, since we were working on a similar time frame. Not collaborating would have made the process more daunting; working together kept us going.**❞**
>
> —NBCT, EARLY CHILDHOOD GENERALIST

The main point of working together is to have additional sets of eyes examining your evidence and asking questions about your assumptions, claims, and choices. Answering questions (whether during a collaborative session or later on your own) can do a few things: (1) Help you explain (and take credit for) choices you might not have clearly explained, (2) help you "see" choices or interactions you may not have noticed, and (3) help you rethink some unexamined assumptions you might have made. A key aspect in the effectiveness of learning communities is the quality of questions asked, so it is worth spending a bit of time learning about the types of questions one can ask and the purposes of each.

When involved in collaborative discussion about evidence from your practice, most questions that are generated fall into two main categories: clarifying questions and probing questions (National School Reform Faculty, n.d.). Clarifying questions seek to clarify the context and typically require a simple, short reporting of facts. Many of the questions in the Instructional Context portion and some of the questions in the Instructional Planning portion of the portfolio are clarifying questions. For example, "What are the number, ages, and grades of the students in class?" is a clarifying question. These questions generally set the stage for the second, more challenging type of question.

Probing questions are designed to stimulate thinking. As such, they require some thought to answer. Probing questions occur throughout the portfolio entries, as they are the heart of the reflective process. For example, "Why is discussion a particularly useful teaching approach for addressing your goals for this lesson?" is a probing question.

Your learning community may find it useful to start a discussion of evidence with clarifying questions. These will help define the context of the learning sequence from which the evidence was generated and serve as "warmup" questions for the group before moving into the mental heavy lifting that comes with probing inquiries. Additionally, clarifying questions often lead to probing questions. Consider this exchange between two candidates:

1   *Kathy:* So, did you assign students to groups, or did they get to choose?

2   *Marie:* I let them choose.

3   *Kathy:* Why did you let them choose?

4   *Marie:* I think they need to exercise some degree of freedom and choice.
5   They need to practice good decision making, so this is one way.

6   *Kathy:* Why is decision making an important skill for students this age?

7   *Marie:* Well, decision making is something they will carry with them into
8   every class and beyond into adulthood. Life is full of decisions and
9   consequences. It is one of the important "secret" things we teach, or should
10   teach, in school beyond content.

11 *Kathy:* OK, so does letting the students choose always work? I mean, are
12   there ever any problems with groups getting off task?

13 *Marie:* Sure, sometimes they do, but that is a consequence of poor decision
14   making. They need to feel a consequence in order to learn to make better
15   decisions.

16 *Kathy:* So, what is the consequence?

17 *Marie:* Maybe a group of friends chooses to work together, and one friend
18   who is kind of flaky doesn't get her work done. The group gets a lower
19   grade. That's the consequence. Next time, maybe the group will think
20   twice about allowing that student in their group.

21 *Kathy:* So, what kind of dynamic does that set up in class?

22 *Marie:* What do you mean?

23 *Kathy:* What I'm hearing is that you expect children this age to be able to
24   stand up to a friend in their social group and say, "No, you can't be in
25   our group." How might that impact the dynamics in your class?

26 *Marie:* Hmmm. I hadn't thought about it that way.

27 *Kathy:* Is there a way to allow students choice but provide some structure
28   or safeguards to reduce the likelihood of conflict, or to allow students to
29   be proactive about preventing or dealing with problems before there is a
30   serious consequence?

Can you identify the clarifying questions and probing questions? Lines 1 and 16 contain clarifying questions because the answers required are short and factual in nature. However, each of these sets up a string of probing questions that follow. The question about grouping in line 1 is followed by two why questions about Marie's rationale for the instructional choices made. The clarifying question about consequences in line 16 is followed by another series of probing queries that push Marie to think about the possible impact of the instructional choices made.

It is worth noticing in line 27 that Kathy does not jump in with advice or a solution but instead poses a question that puts the responsibility back on Marie. Through this dialogue, Kathy is helping Marie recognize a potential instructional dilemma (a dilemma of which she perhaps was not aware) and is given ideas to use for further reflection about this on her own. This is the power of a well-functioning learning community engaged in productive discussion guided by the National Board portfolio process.

⚠ Admittedly, when questions arise about another's teaching practices it can be difficult to refrain from jumping in with answers, suggestions, or even evaluative statements. However, just as it is effective pedagogy to allow space for your students to develop their own thinking and understanding, it is an essential aspect of professional dialogue to provide colleagues the opportunity to process and develop insights into their instructional challenges. Your role as a collaborative peer is to help them identify these challenges and support them in arriving at their own solutions that fit their teaching style and the needs of their students. It shows concern and respect for their learning process to keep asking questions that probe and promote further thinking. And when the conversation turns to your work you will appreciate the reciprocity.

So, what might these sorts of questions look like? Following is a list of sample questions to refer to while meeting with colleagues. It is not exhaustive, but may give your group some ideas to build from.

- What do these students need to know?
- Based on your professional knowledge and experience, why is this important for students to know?
- Does this skill or knowledge transfer to other contexts? How?
- What approach did you use to teach this?
- Why is this approach effective for your students?
- How does this activity help students develop or learn?
- What do you want the students to learn by doing this?
- Why do you think the student said or did that?
- Who is learning? How can you tell?
- What did the student learn? How can you tell?
- What impact did this decision have on learning?
- What did you expect to happen with this lesson?
- What would you change or not change about the lesson and why?

Types and Purposes of Writing

The National Board identifies three types of thinking and writing: descriptive, analytic, and reflective. It is important to recognize the purpose of each. Think back to the phases of reflection: framing and focusing evidence, noticing and identifying evidence, analyzing evidence, and acting on evidence. How do these phases align with the types of writing required in the portfolio entries? Table 4.1 provides one way to think about this relationship.

Descriptive Writing

The purpose of *descriptive* writing is to do just that: describe what transpired. What is the learning goal? What learning activities did you plan? What did the students

TABLE 4.1 Reflection, Writing, and the NBPTS Portfolio

Phase of Reflection	Type of Writing	Location in Portfolio Entry
Framing and focusing evidence	Descriptive	Instructional Context, Instructional Planning
Noticing and identifying evidence	Descriptive	Analysis of Instruction & Student Work; Video Recording Analysis
Analyzing evidence	Analytic	Analysis of Instruction & Student Work; Video Recording Analysis
Acting on evidence	Reflection	Reflection

do? How did they do it? What did they say? The object is to paint a picture so the assessor can "see" the classroom, the lesson, or the interaction as if he or she were actually there. Here are some examples:

Sample 1:

There are 30 students in my second period class, 17 girls and 13 boys. Four are identified as English language learners (ELLs), 10 were redesignated as proficient in English at some point in their academic career, and 11 were initially proficient in English. Five students have parents who completed college; the remainder completed some college or less. This class is part of a sophomore-level team, so they are with one another all day and move in a block from teacher to teacher within an interdisciplinary team that includes World History, English, and Graphic Design.

Sample 2:

I asked students to identify which of the three pictures best showed the idea of a "solid" by indicating with their fingers, one, two or three. Picture one showed athletes in a soccer stadium. Picture two showed athletes seated in a bus on their way to a game. Picture three showed the athletes in the locker room preparing for a game. Most students held up two fingers, which indicated the picture of the athletes on the bus. I asked Cindy to explain why she thought that best showed the idea of a solid. She said, "Because they are all sitting super close together." I followed up by asking, "And how is that like a solid?" She responded, "Because the pieces in the solid are close together." I then restated her terminology, "The pieces?" She caught this cue and replied, "The atoms."

Remember, you are not just describing the context, you are describing *evidence*. It is vital that you remain focused on the learning goal(s) and are specific about the evidence you present.

Analytic Writing

The second type of writing is *analytic*. The purpose of this type of writing is to make meaning from the evidence you identified and described. What does the description of the students' actions and words tell you about their development and/or learning?

Sample 3:

When I looked at his arrangement of the base 10 blocks, I could tell Ethan understood multiplication but struggled with the commutative property. For the problem 3×5 he built 3 groups of 5 blocks and correctly counted the total as 15. He then wrote 5×3 but again showed 3 groups of 5 blocks, rather than 5 groups of 3 blocks, and totaled them to 15. He repeated this same error on each of the remaining 4 block problems. He did answer the word problem correctly (when there were no explicit instructions to use the blocks to show the answer). It is unclear if it is the blocks that were getting in his way, or if the real-life context of the problem assisted him.

Sample 4:

Based on the six-trait writing rubric I used to evaluate Edgar's writing assignment, it was apparent that he is making good progress this year with developing ideas and organizing them in a logical manner. His description of his mother's journey from her childhood in Hungary to her immigration to the United States as a teenager was full of compelling moments and kept me engaged until the end! However, his sentences are still simple and often grammatically incomplete. For example, he wrote, "My mother she comes home from work tired."

Notice that descriptive must precede analytic writing: It is in the description where the evidence is provided. The analytic writing makes sense or meaning of the evidence.

Reflective Writing

The third type of writing is *reflective*. The purpose of this type of writing is to come to some actionable conclusions about your findings. You identified a goal, you collected evidence, you made meaning out of the evidence, so now what? What will your next steps be? What will you change? Why will you change it? What improvements do you anticipate from the change? It is equally important to identify what you will not change and why.

Sample 5:

I realize looking back that I should have provided more scaffolding when students did their report to share their group's thinking. I assumed they would know how to structure their argument; it was clear that they did not. I focused solely on the content part in my instruction, and that was effective based on the level of factual and relevant detail they included; but the order in which they presented ideas was muddled. Next time, I will give them some sample skeletons from which they can choose. This should improve the logical flow and help them tie the information together.

Sample 6:

Thinking about my students' work with comparing fractions, I noticed they tended to make equivalent fractions with a common denominator for every problem. While this shows mastery in creating equivalent fractions, it also shows they did not develop enough conceptual understanding of fractions to notice that comparing fractions with a common numerator would have been easier for several of the problems (e.g., comparing 3/7 and 3/5). This makes me wonder how well they truly understand the meaning of numerator and denominator. The next time I teach comparing fractions I will encourage them to develop more than one strategy first and ask them to explain why each works. This will give me a chance to focus on conceptual knowledge. The procedure for creating equivalent fractions with a common denominator will come on day two.

As the analytic writing relied on the evidence presented in descriptive writing, the conclusions one reaches in reflective writing rely on both the evidence presented and the analysis of the evidence. Ultimately these separate pieces will fit together to create a picture of you as a reflective practitioner.

All three types of writing work together to paint a complete picture of a particular learning sequence and your thinking and understanding about it. All three types also revolve around the effective identification and use of evidence, which is the subject of the next chapter. Learning to identify and then analyze and reflect on evidence is at the heart of the National Board Certification process.

Additional Resources

It might be useful to examine videos of teachers you do not know as a means to develop habits of thinking, dialoguing, and writing about teaching. The Teaching Channel website is free and user-friendly and includes a note-taking tool to use while viewing the videos (**www.teachingchannel.org**). Also, **www.learner.org** from the Annenberg Foundation has a great series of teacher videos and video case studies. Both content knowledge and pedagogical strategies are areas of focus.

Writing portfolio entries requires you to be succinct. You have a lot to convey to the reader in a very limited amount of space. William Zinsser's *On Writing Well* (2001; St. Martin's Press) is an excellent guide for this.

MY THOUGHTS

Use this space to record ideas generated from reading this chapter, including the prompts about the four phases of reflection and the three types and purposes of writing.

_____

_____

_____

_____

_____

_____

_____

_____

_____

_____

_____

_____

_____

_____

_____

_____

Looking for Evidence of the Standards

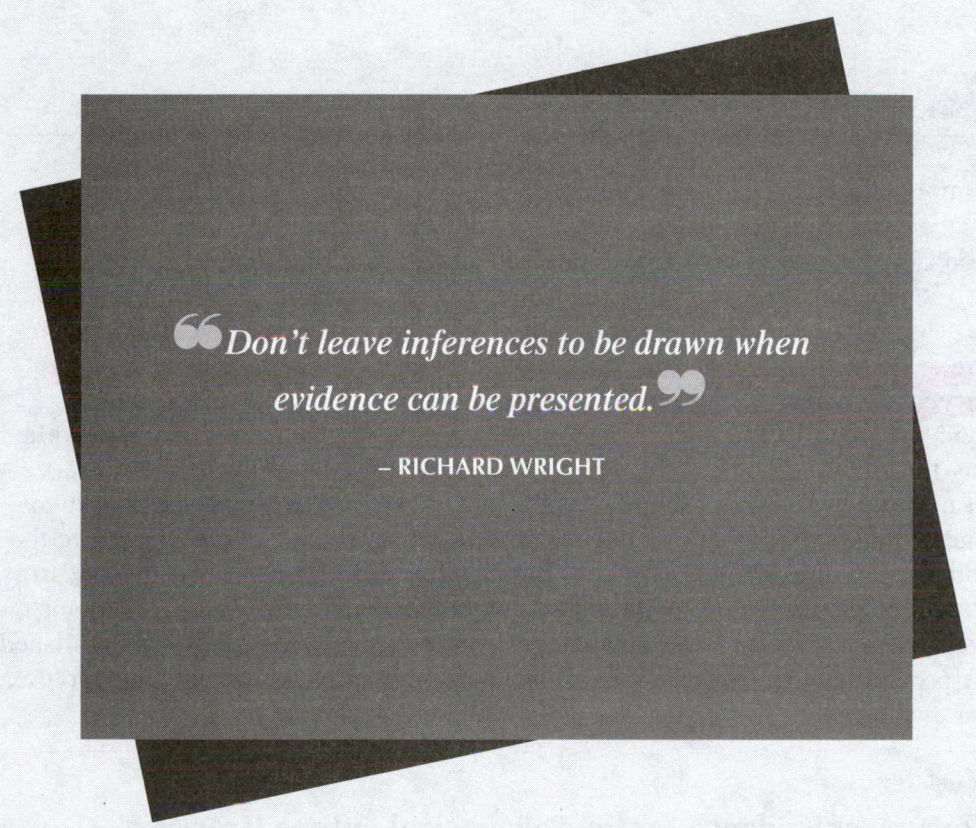

66*Don't leave inferences to be drawn when evidence can be presented.*99

– RICHARD WRIGHT

We hope that in reading this book you have come to realize that the National Board for Professional Teaching Standards (NBPTS), through the Five Core Propositions and the specific certificate standards, establishes a particular set of teaching skills, values, beliefs—a *specific teaching identity.* The entire portfolio is your opportunity to provide clear, consistent, and convincing evidence drawn from your work as a professional that your teaching identity is consistent with that outlined by NBPTS. While you are making claims about how your work as an educator is reflective of the ideas in the core propositions and the certificate standards, the assessors for each of your entries are using an Evaluation of Evidence Guide as they look for scorable evidence. But what is "scorable evidence"?

The process of assessing your portfolio entries is based on a positive scoring system. Points are never subtracted, only added. However, *the assessor can award points only when you provide evidence of meeting the standards listed on the Evaluation of Evidence form that corresponds with each entry*. In this sense, the National Board Certification process is not just about what you did or planned to do, but also about how well you *document and explain* who you are as an educator and *demonstrate the impact* this has on student learning outcomes. The purpose of this chapter, then, is to help clarify what counts as evidence, identify possible sources of evidence, and share ways of writing about evidence. Common errors in the identification, collection, and explanation of evidence will also be addressed. We want you to receive credit where credit is due.

What Counts as Evidence?

Simply put, evidence is something that provides support for a claim or assertion. Rather than thinking about evidence as a binary—either "you have it" or "you don't"—it is more productive to think about each piece of evidence as falling somewhere along a continuum from weak to convincing. Due to the space restrictions of each portfolio entry, it is important you choose the *most convincing* evidence possible to make the case for how your practice as a professional meets the standards of the National Board. What is critical is that whatever evidence you ultimately choose to include in an entry is (a) logically and explicitly linked to a specific claim you are making about how this provides evidence of meeting the National Board standards, (b) described in a way that is easy to understand, and (c) part of a larger set of evidence that collectively points to the same conclusion about your practice as an educator. The goal is for the assessors to see the picture you are painting as closely as how you intend it; you do not want them to have to guess how the pieces fit together. This is best accomplished by providing clear, consistent, and convincing evidence. So, where can you look for evidence?

Sources of Evidence for the Pedagogical Entries (Entries 1–3)

Each entry is designed to assess how well you meet specific standards. Just as you would encourage your students to be aware of what content standards they need to know to prepare for a lesson, learning task, or test, it is critical that you are aware which standards are addressed by each entry. Once this is clear, you can select instructional sequences, and evidence from each sequence, that demonstrate your accomplishment of these standards in a clear, consistent, and convincing way.

While the National Board specifically stipulates the types of evidence for some entries (video, student work), there are still several options open to you. Student work and video evidence are documented differently, so we'll treat each of those in turn in the following sections, but the overall message here is the same: In pedagogical entries, when thinking about evidence selection, consider what will best reveal student thinking and learning and your involvement in creating the conditions that supported student growth and development.

Student Work as Evidence

The purpose of the examination of the student work entry is to demonstrate how well you can:

1. Set appropriate learning goals for all students.
2. Select appropriate materials and activities to help students accomplish these goals.
3. Carry out the designed instruction.
4. Monitor student learning during instruction.
5. Make adjustments to goals and instruction based on how students are learning.
6. Analyze what and how students learned in order to determine next steps and set new learning goals.

In our experience, candidates are typically comfortable with and successful at describing the materials and instruction as initially designed and describing what students knew *before* and *after* an instructional sequence. However, many candidates overlook describing and analyzing *their* role—their actions and choices *during* the instructional sequence. The irony is that this is the most critical part of instruction and the area that distinguishes the highly effective educator. For this reason, evidence about the very practices that the National Board seeks is absent from many candidates' writing and portfolios not because the candidate does not *enact* them, but because the candidate failed to *document* them. In talking with candidates, we find that because monitoring, analyzing, and adjusting *during* instruction is second nature, they are often unconscious of the myriad choices they make in the midst of teaching and thus fail to mention them or are unable to clearly articulate what they know and are able to do and most importantly, why. This is sometimes known as the *expert's blind spot*.

When selecting evidence, think first about the learning goal for the instructional sequence. Sometimes the portfolio instructions are explicit about the type of learning goal; other times you have more freedom to select a learning goal. Be sure to carefully read your portfolio instructions to determine if there are any specific requirements for your entry. It is important to clearly communicate the nature of the learning goal and why it is important, relevant, and appropriate for your learners—all evidence you present about your professional practice and student outcomes should be in relation to this goal.

Once you are clear on the learning goal, describe what you know about your students in relation to this. What do they know, what do they not know, and how do you know this about them? Remember to describe *what this information tells you about what you need to do next.* You want to reveal as much of your professional thinking and decision making as possible.

This leads into the next task of making explicit how the materials and activities you select and design will help your students meet the learning goal. In the way you

> 66*This experience of looking at student work to alter how I teach my students is powerful. It is easy to just turn a blind eye to what I am actually doing and assume it works. That way, I wouldn't have to take responsibility for my actions; it would be the students' fault. Even if I practiced this on a small, personal scale, I would still reap the benefits of better designing my lessons, and ultimately become a better teacher . . . a teacher who learns from experience.*99
>
> —NBCT, EARLY ADOLESCENCE ENGLISH LANGUAGE ARTS

write, be "visible" about your role in what is taking place in the learning environment. For example, rather than writing "Students read Gary Soto's *Buried Onions,*" you might write "I selected *Buried Onions* as the text because its protagonist is someone to whom my students can relate, particularly with respect to the idea that choices that appear simple often are quite complex and require much thought." This provides evidence of your professional decision making. The same goes for the selection of activities. If you have students work in groups of three, explain why that is most appropriate. If you have students keep a learning journal, explain why. If you have students complete practice problems independently, explain why. The *why* is where your thinking as an effective teacher is made visible to the assessors.

Along the way, while students are engaged in the instruction you designed, you likely are collecting information to monitor their progress. Again, you want to make this visible within your portfolio entries. Are you informally questioning students, assessing or evaluating their work as your circulate around the room, taking anecdotal records, polling with a thumbs up or down? What are some formal ways you're monitoring their progress—paper-and-pencil assessments, presentations, visual representations, oral responses, one-on-one conferences? It is important that you explain these information-gathering strategies, what they help you understand about students' learning, and *what actions you took as a result.* While most teachers can follow a lesson plan, effective teachers routinely gather information about student learning and make appropriate adjustments to the lesson plan in the moment. Remember to document these actions.

Finally, at the end of the instructional sequence, what measures did you use to determine student progress *toward the stated goals*? Why did you select these particular measures, and what did students' responses tell you about what they did and did not learn? How does this end point compare with where they started? In what ways did they grow and in what ways did they not grow as much as you would have liked *in relation to your stated goals*? At this point, you might make connections to your instructional choices to reflect on how these influenced student progress toward the goals. If student A learned how to use transitions more consistently in her writing, what did *you* do to create the conditions that allowed for this learning to happen? Conversely, if student B still struggles with the difference between adding and multiplying fractions, what evidence do you see in the student's work that can help you understand the source of the misconception? What specifically is problematic for these students? Was there something in the instruction you designed that contributed to this misunderstanding (either through commission or omission)? From the perspective of the National Board, any evaluation of the effectiveness of your instruction can be done only by examining what you know and are able to do to impact student learning and achievement. Analyze the evidence of learning and progress toward the goal(s) first, then analyze how your teaching helped students get there.

Now it's time to reflect on your analysis and explain your next steps. What new goals will you set and why? What do you need to do to advance student learning and why? *Be sure that the modifications and adjustments you propose are related to and consistent with evidence from your analysis.* We've seen a candidate describe how having students work in pairs was effective and appropriate for a specific learning goal with evidence supporting that claim, who then in the reflection proposed having students work in larger groups the next time. What is it that led to this suggestion that seems inconsistent with the evidence presented? Without such context a key piece of information is left out, making it harder for assessors to get a complete picture of your practice. Similarly, candidates sometimes analyze student progress toward a learning goal and then propose modifications to the lesson that are unrelated to the analysis. The point: Stay focused on your goals and your evidence throughout the description, analysis, and reflection on your work. As a friendly reminder, the large arrow running along the top of our Evidence Evaluation Guide from Chapter 4 cues you to do just that.

So, knowing the task in front of you, think about what student work will provide the richest evidence of learning. What work can best illustrate how student understanding changes as a result of your instruction? What sort of work can provide the best insight into the cause(s) of student errors or student success? It is worth mentioning that though multiple-choice items may be a quick measure of where students are, they are not always very rich as a source for determining how deeply students understand concepts compared to longer constructed-response items. However, data from multiple-choice assessments can be revealing if you go beyond the simple descriptive statistics (percentage correct, average grade, number missed, etc.) and look for patterns of missed or skipped items both within a single student's exam and across a class of students. Do all students skip or miss the same item(s)? Do all students manage to select the same wrong answer for a given problem or type of problem? Responses to these questions are revealing bits of information that can help you target areas for further examination through other means. Perhaps after noting students having trouble with a particular set of items you follow up by having them write out their reasoning to determine how deeply students understand a concept or where their misconceptions lie, or explore other assessment measures.

Once you have selected some rich pieces of evidence, you now need to determine how best to present this evidence in your portfolio. Some entries have specific instructions on how work should be included, so the portfolio instructions should always be your first source for direction. Your portfolio instructions offer some suggestions, so read them carefully. The thought to keep in mind is what will best reveal the richness of student understanding in the work. *Remember, the purpose here is not simply to show that the work was completed but, rather, to document what the work says about what students know, are able to do, or are are not able to do and to explain how this informs your actions and decision-making as an educator.*

Now that you know how to tackle evidence in the form of student work, it is time to move on to consider how to use required video recordings as a source of evidence.

Video as Evidence

Nothing strikes more fear into the heart of a National Board candidate than the thought of being videotaped! Recording yourself can be logistically challenging, the viewing emotionally frustrating, and the analysis time-consuming; however, the benefits of video analysis are plentiful and well documented. Teacher reflections completed solely from memory are often more superficial, more general, and less likely to focus on student thinking as compared to reflections completed when the same teachers have access to a video of their teaching (Rosaen, Lundeberg, Cooper, Fritzen, & Terpstra, 2008). Video of your interactions with students and between students allows for multiple viewings and the slowing down of events of interest. When student voices are clearly audible on the clip and the task students are engaged in is well designed, evidence will be jumping out at you from the screen.

Like the student work in the student work entry, the video in the video entries is a source of evidence. Note that the video itself does not get scored—it is your written analysis and response to what the video shows about the interactions, teaching, and learning that occurred (including before, during, and after the clip) that will be closely examined by the assessor. When recording your video, there is no need for perfection; just teach a solid lesson. For full candidates, typically two of the four portfolio entries require video evidence (but double-check your portfolio instructions to be sure because this may not always be the case). The length and focus of the videos vary—some are 20 minutes, some are 10, some require the students to be in small groups, some require the use of manipulatives, etc. It is critical that you understand the specific requirements for your video before you attempt to analyze and write. You will not be able to provide evidence of supporting students working in small groups if there are no small groups in your video. The portfolio entry instructions include suggestions to help you make good choices in selecting what to feature in your videos. Use that resource and refer back to it often.

> 66 *My first reaction to seeing myself on video was, "Wow! Do I really sound like that?" The first few times I was nit-picking everything. But after the second, third, or maybe the thirtieth time I was able to get beyond that. It was then I realized all the really good things that had happened during the lesson that I hadn't been aware of before.* 99
>
> —NBCT, ADOLESCENCE AND YOUNG ADULTHOOD ENGLISH LANGUAGE ARTS

When it comes to analyzing what you've recorded, many of the same strategies previously mentioned in the student work section apply here. The assessors are looking for your Architecture for Accomplished Teaching (or as our model depicts it, the Cycle of High-Impact Teaching). Do you set high, worthwhile, and meaningful goals? Do you design and implement appropriate assessments and instruction in light of those goals? Do you monitor progress toward those goals and make appropriate adjustments in light of what you learn about how students are progressing? Do you determine reasonable next steps? Again, be explicit and clear about your decision making at each step. Use the Evidence Evaluation Guide from Chapter 4 to help you understand what the video interactions tell you about student learning and how your instructional choices played a role.

One strategy we've found helpful with video entries is taking the time to write out a transcript for your video. This is time-consuming, but it offers some important benefits. First, it allows you to really get to know your video because you will have to watch it multiple times to create the transcript. Because you are writing what you and students say word-for-word, it forces you to pay close attention to the thinking captured in the video and allows for in-depth analysis. You may find that you missed a question or comment a student asked when just watching the video, but it stands out when actually typing it out. Second, having the transcript completed makes selecting direct quotes to use as evidence in your entry much easier. Since the dialogue is already written up, you can quickly read through and select the most powerful segments to include in your writing. But, remember: Support these direct quotes with an interpretation of what they mean in relation to the teaching and learning for the instructional sequence. Why are the quotes or dialogue significant? What do they tell you about student learning? Quotes without analysis will not demonstrate to the assessor that you are able to monitor and reason about student thinking.

One of the most important elements in completing the video entries is obtaining signed student release forms. Since getting the forms returned can sometimes be a challenge, get the release forms sent out early! Remember to secure signed releases for any adults appearing in video segments also. We recommend using the materials from NBPTS to draft a letter to send home with the forms to explain the purpose of the video to parents or caregivers. Have your principal or site administrator look it over and approve before sending the letter home. This will ensure your administrator is aware of what you are doing and may open the door for increased support. Consider phoning parents and guardians who refuse to grant permission for their child to be in the video to talk with them about National Board Certification, why you are pursuing it, and the impact it will have on their child's learning. Sometimes, a simple explanation of the purpose of the recording is enough to ease their concerns. However, if you do have students in your classroom who cannot appear in the video, consider moving them to a common location in the room or another classroom during the video recording. Let your videographer know that those students may not appear on video. Or, if you are using a static camera location, adjust the camera angle so that they will not appear in the shot.

Last, some technical advice: Be sure to read the section in Part I of your portfolio instructions on recording video. It includes useful information about equipment and camera angles that will increase the likelihood of capturing the type of evidence you need to write about in your entries. You may want to consider buying (or borrowing) an external microphone to capture student voices or simply repeating or paraphrasing what students say—particularly those who are soft-spoken, shy, or nonnative English speakers. In general, a static camera location is OK for a large-group video, but for any small-group videos find someone who can hand-carry the camera around to the groups. This will greatly improve the likelihood you can hear what the students are saying. The camera can stay with one group for the entire segment, or have the cameraperson move it between groups as directed by your portfolio instructions. In any case, make sure the person who is recording understands the type of evidence you are looking for.

Additionally, make sure your videographer understands any special requirements of the specific entry. For some entries *pausing and restarting the recording isn't permissible.* Fire alarms go off, announcements come on over the intercom, and visitors come into the room but keep the camera rolling! The assessors are experienced educators themselves; they understand what occurs in the school setting. The quality of your analysis is what is important, not whether your video was free from everyday distractions. It is OK to use a segment with a disruption in the middle if you think the evidence that occurs before and after are great. You may be able to select a clip that does not "feature" a disruption, but it is heartbreaking for candidates to lose a quality interaction because the videographer stopped recording. For example, during one author's (Leslee's) video a parent came into her room and Leslee motioned to her videographer to keep recording. What could have been a problem was a benefit because the parent simply sat down and started working with her child and his peers at his table. All the children remained on task because they were accustomed to visits like this. What great evidence of the parent–family connection standard! Of course, Leslee remembered to get a release form signed by the parent afterward (yes, even adults need to sign those). Our point—keep the camera rolling.

One last comment about recording: If you are hoping to lead off your video with a great interaction, be sure to leave a bit of cushion at the start of the video recording. Sometimes, in the process of the camera starting up, the first few seconds of the video are cut short or not seen or heard clearly. The same can be said for interactions that occur at the very end of your recording. Begin your video recording a few seconds early and end a few moments after the conclusion of your lesson to be sure to capture all that you might want to use for your entry.

When you've decided what segment or segments to use in your entry, it is time to get these into a separate location. Some candidates are capable of extracting clips and assembling their own videos, but it is also acceptable to get outside help. More than a few candidates we've worked with asked digitally savvy students to help them. Just as you need to coach your videographer about the do's and don'ts, you will want to make sure whoever is putting together your video understands what is acceptable and unacceptable. For example, the portfolio instructions make clear that techniques such as fade-outs, transitions, subtitles, and the like are not allowed. However well intentioned these enhancements may be, they will make your video invalid.

Sometimes, despite all precautions, videos do not turn out as you hoped. Be proactive. Start recording early and often. This will desensitize you and your students to being on camera. The result will be a more natural classroom environment when you do record. These early recordings will allow you to troubleshoot audio problems and determine the best camera angles. Plan to record multiple lessons so you have choices about what to use for your entry. You do not want to be scrambling before the submission deadline without a viable recording. And, of course, make a backup. Another author's (Tara's) Entry 3 VHS tape broke while rewinding it the night before the submission day! Fortunately, she had the master and was able to make a duplicate. This process is stressful enough without having to contend with failed technology—keep multiple copies of *everything*.

While the video entries are often the most feared, the seemingly straight-forward documented accomplishments entry is also deserving of your careful attention. Time to learn about Entry 4.

Sources of Evidence for the Documented Accomplishments Entry (Entry 4)

This is probably the most misinterpreted entry among the four that are required. Let's start with what this entry is *not*: a long list of awards, degrees, and certifications earned; titles and positions held; conferences and events attended; or courses taken. Rather, the intent of the documented accomplishments entry is for you to identify accomplishments that are reflective of the National Board standards and describe how these impacted student learning. These should be evidence of what you do beyond the norm of everyday teaching or usual school activities such as open house. These are actions that are instrumental in your being an effective teacher.

There are three categories of accomplishments you must provide evidence for:

1. You as a leader or collaborator
2. You as a learner
3. You as a partner with parents or the community

Even though they may occur beyond the four walls of a classroom setting, they absolutely impact how and what happens inside it to support student learning. Each one of your accomplishments must be linked to how it influences student learning, whether it be your own students or those of colleagues. Remember, too, that as with the other entries, the impact on student learning can be implied or described as what you expect to happen in the future as a result of your actions.

Like the other entries, there are specific standards the National Board identifies and it is critical that you read and understand what evidence the assessors will look for. When identifying your accomplishments, think about what actions you have taken that best exemplify the National Board standards. When writing up your accomplishments, think about evidence that documents not only that the accomplishment occurred, but also how it impacted student learning.

An example may help you understand what types of accomplishments yield more convincing evidence of the standards. Let's say you write and send a class newsletter home to your students' families. This demonstrates one way you reach out to parents (good), but a closer read of the National Board standards indicates that communication with families should be two way and treat caregivers as partners (better!). What evidence about the type of communication and relationship with families does this newsletter provide? Do you get comments or questions back from caregivers after sending out the newsletter? Do you write the newsletter by yourself, or do caregivers or students help write part of it? The point: It isn't so much the newsletter itself but how it serves as a tool to foster dialogue and build relationships with families. With this in mind, the focus of your description of the newsletter should be about how it helps generate dialogue and build relationships. Should you include a copy of the newsletter as your artifact or e-mails or notes from families about how they used information from the newsletter to support their child's learning? What provides better evidence of the standards? And finally, remember the connection to student learning. How does this newsletter and the dialogue and relationships it supports impact student learning? Are children who hear their caregiver expressing interest in what is going on at school more likely to see school as important and learn more? It is important to make this last connection back to the classroom when documenting accomplishments.

Let's take another example: you as a leader. Perhaps you've served on a district curriculum committee. Do you provide copies of agendas noting your presence at the meetings, or do you provide evidence of the impact your activities had on student learning? Maybe you can show data or anecdotes indicating student growth as a result of the work the committee did? Remember, it isn't so much about the accomplishment itself, but the *impact* of the accomplishment.

You might be starting to see, with these earlier examples, that two candidates could write up the same accomplishment but paint two very different pictures if one focuses on the evidence of the accomplishment occurring and the other focuses on the evidence of the accomplishment's *impact*. Help ensure that you are the candidate who writes about the impact of your accomplishments, not just an archiver of experiences, by reading the National Board standards carefully and thinking about the focus of your evidence when you document your accomplishment.

At the time of this writing, candidates were allowed to document up to eight accomplishments. This does not leave much room to elaborate. It is our opinion that it may be better to document fewer accomplishments well rather than many accomplishments superficially. We often have candidates start writing up several accomplishments. It usually becomes clear early on in the writing process that some accomplishments are easier to connect to student learning than others. When using the scoring guide the National Board makes available on its website, some accomplishments "pop" with evidence and others not so much. At that point, the accomplishments that are not yielding as much evidence are eliminated to free up more space for other, richer accomplishments. Quality is more important than quantity.

Writing About Evidence

⚠ It is one thing to be able to identify and analyze evidence, but it is another to be able to clearly communicate to others what that evidence reveals about learning and achievement of instructional goals. We have worked with excellent teachers who failed to certify, not because they were ineffective teachers but because they did not adequately document and explain evidence of their expertise. Some specific errors have been mentioned previously, but it is worth reiterating some of the more common ones. The three most common weaknesses we have seen in candidate's writing are:

1. Failing to write with knowledge of the National Board standards
2. Relying on the assessor to make inferences about your instructional choices made during the planning, enactment, and analysis of an instructional sequence
3. Relying on the assessor to make inferences about the impact of your actions on student learning.

Writing to the National Board Standards

As mentioned earlier in this chapter, assessors are limited to what is on the scoring guide. They cannot award points for claims for which you do not provide evidence. Read the standards carefully. Know them intimately. The whole National Board process is an assessment measuring your achievement of these standards. If a candidate does not provide clear, consistent, and convincing evidence of the standards in their entries and assessment center responses, it is unlikely he or she will earn enough points to certify. This process is about being able to articulate what you know and are able to do as a high-impact teacher.

Some support providers encourage candidates to directly quote the language of the standards in your entry. There is nothing wrong with cuing the assessor that you are attempting to show evidence of a particular standard by using the language of the National Board. If you think about it, the assessors are reading entries of multiple candidates, so anything you can do to make it easier to identify evidence helps. Our caution is this: *Citing a standard is not evidence of accomplishing the standard.* Seeing the language of the standard may tip off the assessor that you are about to provide some evidence, but if clear, consistent, and convincing evidence of that standard does not follow, you will not earn points.

Taking Credit for Your Choices

Do not leave room for inference—be clear about your motives for why a specific set of learning objectives was appropriate for your students at that particular time; be clear about your rationale for the instructional choices you employed in the strategies and activities you designed to support your students in learning; and be clear about which students did and did not learn, what was learned and not learned and how you know. Let's take these recommendations one at a time.

Taking Credit for Your Choices About Curriculum

Many educators these days are provided with some documentation or external expectations of what must be taught and learned in a given academic year. However, to establish that you meet National Board standards it is not enough to say you taught a particular set of objectives at a specific point in the school year simply because the state, a professional organization, or the school board determined these must be in the curriculum. You must explain why these learning objectives are important for students' growth or development. Think about it this way—why did the state, school board, or professional organization identify this particular set of concepts or skills as important? And why does a specific set of objectives come just after or just before another? Rather than appearing to have a passive role in establishing your curriculum, show that you take an active stance. For example, here is a passive versus an active way to discuss curricular choices:

> The state standards require that all students be able to describe America's pre-Columbian settlements. [Passive: No evidence of curricular rationale.]

> *versus*

> Students should be familiar with America's pre-Columbian settlements because the government and culture of these communities influenced early colonists' ideas about federal government and later became cultures that created challenges to efforts to expand colonial settlements westward. [Active: Clear rationale for the purpose of the content and how it connects with other learning.]

Which sounds more like a thoughtful, mindful practitioner who is aware of how current learning objectives connect to later important curricular themes?

Additionally, though the curricular goals for the year may not be up to you, the way in which the curriculum is sequenced and how it is taught might be. If you decided to teach fraction addition before decimal addition, explain why. If you teach narrative writing before expository writing, explain why. If you explain genetics before evolution, discuss why. Your rationale should be grounded in the certificate standards, your knowledge of how students learn best, your insights into the broader curriculum to inform instructional sequences that promote conceptual coherence, and your knowledge of your particular group of students (cognitively and socioemotionally) at that point in the instructional year.

Taking Credit for Your Choices About Instructional Strategies

Students do not *magically* end up in groups—you chose to put them there. Manipulatives do not *magically* end up in students' hands—you chose to provide them. Directions or diagrams do not *magically* end up projected on the screen for everyone to see—you chose to project them. These may be important choices you made as a professional that contribute to the success of your lesson and, more importantly, your students' learning. Write actively about them. Consider the following:

> Students worked in pairs to complete the problems on the worksheet.

> *versus*

> At this point in the instructional sequence, students need to practice the problem-solving strategy through working problems. I provided a worksheet with some sample problems for students to work through. Knowing that students often need to be able to not only complete problems, but also be able to

explain the problem-solving process, I grouped students in pairs so they could discuss their strategies.

Both describe the same event, but the intentions and decisions of the teacher are much more "active" in the second example. They are written in such a way that an assessor can clearly see the teacher's decision-making and how this impacts student learning.

Identifying and Taking Credit for Student Learning

The basis of any analysis of instructional effectiveness is determining *who* learned, *what* was learned, and *how well* it was learned. Only then can you examine and evaluate the contributing actions of the instructor. If this evidence about *who, what,* and *how well* is not available, rigorous analysis of the impact of the teacher is not possible. Evidence gathering is an intentional and active process and the quantity and quality of evidence available for analysis is strongly related to lesson design. Ask yourself these questions:

- What opportunities do students have to show what they know and how well they know it? Through writing? Through speaking? Through drawing? Through moving?

- How visible are these student outcomes to you as the instructor, either in the course of instruction or after the fact? Can you hear individual students? Can you read their writing? Can you see what they are drawing and doing?

- What opportunities do you have to respond to this visible student thinking and provide feedback?

- How did your actions and choices contribute to what was learned and not learned?

Some candidates can identify what was learned but are not clear about how what is was they did that impacted student learning. These teacher "moves," as they are sometimes called, are not always easy to see. In many cases, they run in the background. Much of the hard work of effective teaching occurs before the students even enter the classroom. It is built into the activities and resources you select, the time you allot and the structure and environment you build for these experiences to take place. The choice of one novel that students really identify with over one that does not resonate with them may make a difference in how much learning occurs. The type, timing, and mode of feedback you provide to students also make a difference. Are you adjusting your plans in response to evidence of student learning? These adjustments matter and your ability to document them clearly, consistently, and convincingly makes a huge difference in whether assessors will have evidence of your effective practice!

Making Student Thinking Visible

Student work and videos of practice are like mines and evidence is the ore. Some mines are rich in ore; others not so much. Some of the ore is buried deep and requires a lot of digging to find; others have abundant veins near the surface.

Obviously, you want to work in a mine with abundant and easily accessible ore rather than one where you must expend a lot of effort and obtain a small yield. You, as the designer of the instruction, have control over this. Think about the previous questions while *designing* your instruction and *build in opportunities to make evidence of student thinking visible*. Not only will it make the writing of your portfolio easier, it will likely make you an even more responsive instructor.

Video Analysis Example

Consider this exchange between a support provider and two social studies candidates as they review lesson videos (the transcripts are provided for you). The content goals of the lesson are to "identify the locations of human communities that populated the major regions of the world and describe how humans adapted to a variety of environments." Think about what evidence for the standards you can identify from the lesson as it is described.

1   *Maria* [*support provider*]: OK, Bill, what do we need to know
2   about this lesson before we look for evidence?

3   *Bill* [*candidate*]: Well, this was a lesson where I did some direct
4   instruction on the names and locations of the ancient civiliza-
5   tions, then got the students into groups and had them label a map
6   of the ancient world using their notes. Each group member had a
7   job, and to help some of the students with their oral reporting, I
8   encouraged them to use the sentence stems. They each get a set
9   of these and I put them on a pink sheet of paper so they are easy
10   to find in their notebook. So, this part of the video is the report-
11   ing out after the group work.

12   *Maria:* OK, so we all have the evaluation of evidence guide in
13   front of us. Let's take a look and see what evidence can be iden-
14   tified in this clip. [*Video starts*]

15   *Bill:* OK, ladies and gentlemen. Let's go over together what you
16   did on your maps. What ancient civilization was located here, at
17   area A? [*teacher displays a regional map with different-colored*
18   *shaded area on a document camera and points to shaded area*
19   *labeled "A," waits 5 seconds, and rolls a die*] OK, 3. The die of
20   destiny says group 3 goes first here. [*smiles*] Who's the spokes-
21   person for group 3?

22   *Sun:* That's me.

23   *Bill:* OK, Jill. What did your group come up with for this
24   question?

25   *Sun:* The ancient Egyptians.

26   *Bill:* Use your reporting stems to speak in a complete sentence
27   please.

28   *Sun:* [*referring to a pink sheet of paper on her desk*] Um, my
29   group agreed that the ancient Egyptians lived at A.

30   *Bill:* Great. Does everyone agree? Thumbs up or down? [*all but a*
31   *few students give the thumbs up sign*] OK. And what river runs
32   through area A, group 3?

33 *Sun:* The Nile River.

34 *Bill:* [*holds up pink paper with reporting stems*]

35 *Sun:* [*looking at her pink paper*] Um, we decided that the Nile
36   River goes through area A.

37 *Bill:* Great. Thumbs up or down, everyone? [*all but a few stu-*
38   *dents give the thumbs up sign*] Nice job. OK, area B. Who lived
39   there? [*points at map and rolls die*] 5! OK, group 5, who is your
40   spokesperson?

41 *Jack:* I am. [*raises hand*]

42 *Bill:* All right, whaddya got?

43 *Jack:* Our group concurs that the Sumerians lived in area B.
44   [*speaking in a "serious" voice, like a businessperson or*
45   *attorney*]

46 *Bill:* [*smiles*] All right. Everyone agree or disagree? [*all but a*
47   *few students give the thumbs up sign*] Evan, Janel, Micah,
48   what do you guys think, thumbs up or down? [*Evan, Janel,*
49   *and Micah join the class in showing a thumbs up sign*] OK.
50   Thanks.

51 *Jack:* And the rivers in that area are the Tigris and Euphrates
52   Rivers. [*again with the serious voice*]

53 *Bill:* Ahh, yes. Thank you, sir. What does everyone think about
54   that? Correct? [*all students give a thumbs up*] Great. OK,
55   and super bonus question. What is area B also called? It has
56   a special name. [*traces a curve with his finger over area B on*
57   *the map*]

58 *Class:* [*several students shouting*] Fertile Crescent!

59 *Bill:* Great! You guys are so smart! OK, moving on to area C.
60   [*rolls die*] Group 4! Your spokesperson?

61 *Jaime:* That's me.

62 *Bill:* OK. Who lived in area C?

63 *Jaime:* My group agreed that the ancient Indians lived in
64   group C.

65 *Bill:* And . . .

66 *Jamie:* . . . And that the river they lived near was the Indus
67   River.

68 *Bill:* All right. Is there only one river in area C?

69 *Danielle:* No.

70 *Bill:* OK, Danielle. I agree with you, but are you the spokesperson
71   for your group?

72 *Jaime:* There are two rivers. The other one is, uh [*looks at map*]
73   Gan–, Gang– . . .

74 *Bill:* Ganges?

75 *Jaime:* Yeah.

76 *Bill:* That's a tough one to pronounce. Does everyone agree? [*most*
77   *students give a thumbs up*] OK, so we've got three civilizations,

78 all around a river. Great. One more. Group 1, you are left. What
79 do you have for area D?

80 *Sean:* The ancient Chinese civilization lived in area D. It has two
81 rivers, just like area C.

82 *Bill:* Just like the Indus valley, OK. And they are?

83 *Sean:* The Huang and the Chang.

84 *Bill:* Complete sentence, please.

85 *Sean:* Um, the rivers are the Huang and the Chang Rivers.

86 *Bill:* Great, so all four of these ancient civilizations are around
87 important rivers. The Egyptians, the Sumerians, the Indians, and
88 the Chinese. [*pointing at each area on the map in turn*] Fantastic
89 work, everyone. [*Video ends*]

90 *Maria:* All right. Lisa, what do you notice?

91 *Lisa* [*candidate*]: Well, I like the rapport you have with your stu-
92 dents, but I want to know more about the dice—why do you use
93 that to call on groups?

94 *Bill:* Yeah, "the die of destiny." I use that to choose groups
95 randomly, so I don't call on groups in a predictable pattern.
96 Sometimes if I just go right to left across the room, some
97 students tune out, so this keeps their attention up a bit. Plus they
98 think it is kind of fun.

99 *Lisa:* OK, so that and giving each student a job seems like evi-
100 dence of equity, access, and fairness. Everyone contributes.
101 Everyone has their own paper. Everyone has the sentence
102 stems so even if they aren't a great speaker, they have support
103 there.

104 *Bill:* Yeah, some kids I have to remind to use it, but other kids
105 have some fun with it, like Jack there.

106 *Lisa:* Ha. [*smiles*] He seems a bit of a character. But I like how
107 he uses the tool too, even though his spoken English is pretty
108 good. I think that could be evidence of knowledge of your
109 students, knowing that some need that extra lexical support.
110 And making it pink so they can find it among the mess in their
111 folders.

112 *Bill:* Right.

113 *Maria:* So, what evidence do you see for student learning?

114 *Lisa:* Well, each group was able to answer your questions cor-
115 rectly. And, you did the thumbs up thing to check for under-
116 standing with the group.

117 *Bill:* Yeah, that also keeps them engaged.

118 *Lisa:* Did they all complete the map?

119 *Bill:* Pretty much. They were all labeled correctly. That's why I
120 had it on the document camera, so if a group had an error, they
121 could see it and correct it. You know, some were colored neater
122 than others, but I'm mostly concerned with the labels being
123 correct.

124 *Lisa:* Right.

125 *Maria:* So, I want to direct us back to the content goals for this
126   lesson: Identify the locations of human communities that popu-
127   lated the major regions of the world and describe how humans
128   adapted to a variety of environments. So, would you say your
129   students mastered these goals?

130 *Bill:* Well, identifying the locations, yeah, they did that.

131 *Lisa:* The oral report out, the thumbs up, the maps are all evidence
132   that they know those.

133 *Maria:* How about the second part: adapting to a variety of
134   environments?

135 *Bill:* Well, the four communities were in different parts of the
136   world.

137 *Lisa:* Right, but was there a question about that on the map, or after
138   the video?

139 *Bill:* Well, um. No, I guess not. I think I just assumed they'd notice
140   that.

141 *Lisa:* I wonder if they noticed all of these communities are based
142   around a major river?

143 *Bill:* Well, it shows the rivers on the map.

144 *Lisa:* Did anyone mention it, like "hey, these are all near a
145   river"?

146 *Bill:* No. No, they didn't *say* it, but I'm pretty sure they noticed.
147   Also, I said it, I think at the end.

148 *Lisa:* Oh, I didn't catch that.

149 *Maria:* So how strong is the evidence that students achieved the
150   second goal?

151 *Bill:* I don't think it's very strong. OK. Maybe I should have
152   pointed it out more clearly.

153 *Lisa:* Or maybe ask the students what *they* notice that all of the
154   communities have in common. See if *they* can tell you.

155 *Maria:* OK, let's say they get that they are all centered on a major
156   river. Is there evidence that they understand *why*? What is so
157   special about a river for these early communities?

158 *Bill:* Yeah. I guess we didn't talk about that. I don't really know if
159   they got that or not.

160 *Lisa:* That would also be a National Board standard: looking for
161   patterns.

162 *Maria:* OK, and looking at some of the other National Board
163   social science standards, how are students using critical thinking
164   and marshalling evidence?

165 *Bill:* Not so much in this clip. These were mostly recall
166   questions. I could have added some questions to push students'
167   thinking critically. I need to bump my questioning up
168   a bit.

169   *Lisa:* Or find a way to make what the students are thinking more
170   visible on video. They could be thinking all sorts of things, but
171   we don't know.

172   *Bill:* OK. This was helpful. I have some things to consider for my
173   reflection. Thanks.

Bill's video had some clear evidence of meeting standards. Students were able to correctly identify where the civilizations were located, based on oral reports and maps Bill collected. Bill mentioned that each student had an assigned role, and Bill provided some scaffolding for oral reporting. He enforced the use of the sentence stems for reporting and the roles. Both of these structures respond to what he sees as a student need for support in learning to participate orally in whole-class discussions. He used a die to determine which group was to be called on next. Taken together, these strategies provide some evidence of attention to the National Board standard of creating learning environments that are characterized as being safe and promoting equity.

As the conversation about the clip revealed, there are areas where evidence is lacking, too. There is no evidence about how much each group member participated in the decisions about what civilizations lived where. It is also unclear what type of discussion occurred in the small groups around the task. Bill attempted to check for understanding by having students signal agreement or disagreement, but it is unclear how accurately this technique measured understanding. Bill designed what appears to be a simple labeling task that did not afford opportunities for students to analyze the material in a meaningful manner. Bill acknowledges that while he is confident that his students know the locations of the different civilizations, he is less sure about how well students understand the relationship between geographic features and the location of these civilizations.

Because Bill and his colleagues took the time to analyze the clip deeply by focusing on evidence, areas of strength and areas for growth were revealed. This will help Bill better recognize his strengths and identify areas he can work on to improve the content rigor of not only this lesson but subsequent lessons he designs.

Looking at a Student Work Example

Next, consider this sixth-grade student work sample on equivalent fractions shown in Figure 5.1. As you examine it, look for evidence of both the student's understanding of fractions and how this assignment reflects the National Board standards for teachers of mathematics.

What follows is the interaction between Claudia, the teacher who brought this work sample, and her colleague, Linda, who is also a sixth-grade mathematics teacher:

1   *Linda:* I think there is pretty good evidence that this student under-
2   stands equivalent fractions. He got all the problems on the top
3   section correct. He's making little notes about what to multiply
4   or divide by on each problem.

FIGURE 5.1

Sixth Grade Student Work Sample

Find the missing value to make an equal pair.

1.
$$\frac{6}{12} = \frac{3}{6}$$

2.
$$\frac{2}{3} = \frac{6}{9}$$

3.
$$\frac{1}{4} = \frac{3}{12}$$

4.
$$\frac{15}{20} = \frac{3}{4}$$

5.
$$\frac{3}{9} = \frac{6}{18}$$

6.
$$\frac{2}{10} = \frac{6}{30}$$

7.
$$\frac{7}{21} = \frac{1}{3}$$

8.
$$\frac{80}{100} = \frac{8}{10}$$

Write < > or = for each pair.

9.
$$\frac{3}{10} < \frac{4}{20}$$

10.
$$\frac{6}{8} > \frac{1}{3}$$

11.
$$\frac{2}{4} < \frac{8}{16}$$

12.
$$\frac{1}{5} < \frac{2}{3}$$

5 *Claudia:* Right, except number 8. We talk a lot about dividing
6   and multiplying by 10, you know, so I think he just dropped
7   a zero on that one. But, he got only two out of the last four
8   correct.

9 *Linda:* Maybe he just rushed. He still got 10 out of 12. That's
10   pretty good.

11 *Claudia:* Yeah, but look at numbers 9 and 1. Why would he miss
12   *those*? They're easy compared to 10 and 12 which he got right.
13   You just multiply by a whole number factor to get a common
14   denominator. He did this well on the first 8 problems so I don't
15   get it.

16 *Linda:* Huh. You're right. That's weird.

17 *Claudia:* Yeah. There's something going on, but I don't know
18   what it is. I wonder if he's just picking the larger numerators,
19   thinking those fractions must be bigger? I wish I knew what he
20   was thinking!

At first glance, this student appears to do well with the procedure of creating equivalent fractions (items 1–8), providing correct answers for every problem. But his understanding of the meaning of fractions as numbers appears limited since he missed two of the four fraction comparison items. However, Claudia and Linda are left to speculate about the source of his errors because the task did not require the student to provide an explanation or justification for his responses. Justifying and communicating conclusions is one of the National Board standards for teachers of mathematics, but in the way this assignment was designed there was no opportunity to provide evidence of this standard. Likewise, based on this one piece of student work, there is limited evidence of how Claudia might meet the "art of teaching" standard by using a wide range of formats to promote and assess student learning. Her discussion with Linda has helped Claudia uncover this, giving her something to consider as she reflects on her teaching practices through the certification process.

What we want you to take away from these examples is the importance of designing activities and tasks that require students to share their thinking and reasoning. In doing so, there will be a better chance that the student artifacts (e.g., work samples; snippets of in-class conversation) will provide rich evidence about their learning that you can then attribute to your teaching practice. When looking for evidence, it is vital that you go beyond the descriptive statistics and dig into the student thinking behind the work. Think about what Claudia could do to generate student responses that would provide better evidence of their learning. How could she modify this assignment to gain greater insight into this student's errors? Where else might she look for confirming evidence?

In summary, while looking for evidence in videos and student work, think about these questions:

- What are the National Board standards for which you are looking for evidence within this sequence?
- What specific evidence do you see for each standard?
- What specific action—yours or that of your students—supports your claim about meeting a particular standard?
- What are the learning objectives for this sequence?
  - What specific evidence do you see that each objective was met?
  - Who learned? What did they learn? What is the evidence?
  - Who did not learn? What is the evidence?
  - Were errors or misconceptions present? What were they?
- What inferences can you draw from the evidence you provide?
- Does the evidence make sense with respect to the claim(s) you are trying to make about student learning? How about with respect to your stated learning objectives(s)?
- Do you see missed opportunities to enact the National Board standards? What changes could you make?

Now that you have the tools to analyze, put them to work. Stay focused on the instructions, the prompts, and the standards. Build coherent arguments and consistently support them with clear and convincing evidence. In the drafting stage, don't worry too much about the page limits—just write! Get your ideas out there; worry about editing and tightening things up later. It is challenging work, but we think you will find it rewarding and enlightening. When you are done planning, analyzing, writing, and editing you get to begin packing! The next chapter is about preparing to send your work to NBPTS for scoring.

Additional Resources

As you think about evidence of student thinking and learning , you might find it useful to explore resources for teachers provided by the following nonprofit professional organizations:

- International Reading Association (**www.reading.org**)
- International Society for Technology in Education (**www.iste.org/**)
- National Association for Bilingual Education (**www.nabe.org**)
- National Association for Health and Physical Education (**www.aahperd.org/ naspe/**)
- National Association for the Education of Young Children (**www.naeyc.org/**)
- National Council for History Education (**www.history.org/nche**)
- National Council for the Social Studies (**www.ncss.org**)
- National Council for Teachers of English (**www.ncte.org**)
- National Council of Teachers of Mathematics (**www.nctm.org**)
- National Institute for Literacy (**www.nifl.gov**)
- National Science Teachers Association (**www.nsta.org**)
- Partnership for 21st Century Skills (**www.p21.org/**)
- Teachers of English to Speakers of Other Languages (**www.tesol.org**)

The National Archives and the Library of Congress have several resources for exploring primary source documents in the classroom. These sites include DocsTeach (**http://docsteach.org/**); Digital Vault (**www.digitalvaults.org/**); and the Library of Congress teacher site (**www.loc.gov/teachers/**).

An outstanding resource for anyone who teaches science is a website organized by Jessica Thompson at the University of Washington (**http:// tools4teachingscience.org/**). It has tools for promoting discourse within classrooms during teaching and tools for discussion work outside the classroom. Generalist candidates may find the "Big Idea" tool particularly useful.

Use this space to record ideas generated from reading this chapter, including thinking about sources of evidence and writing about evidence.

_____

_____

_____

_____

_____

_____

_____

_____

_____

_____

_____

_____

_____

_____

_____

6

Sending Your Portfolio: Packing the Box

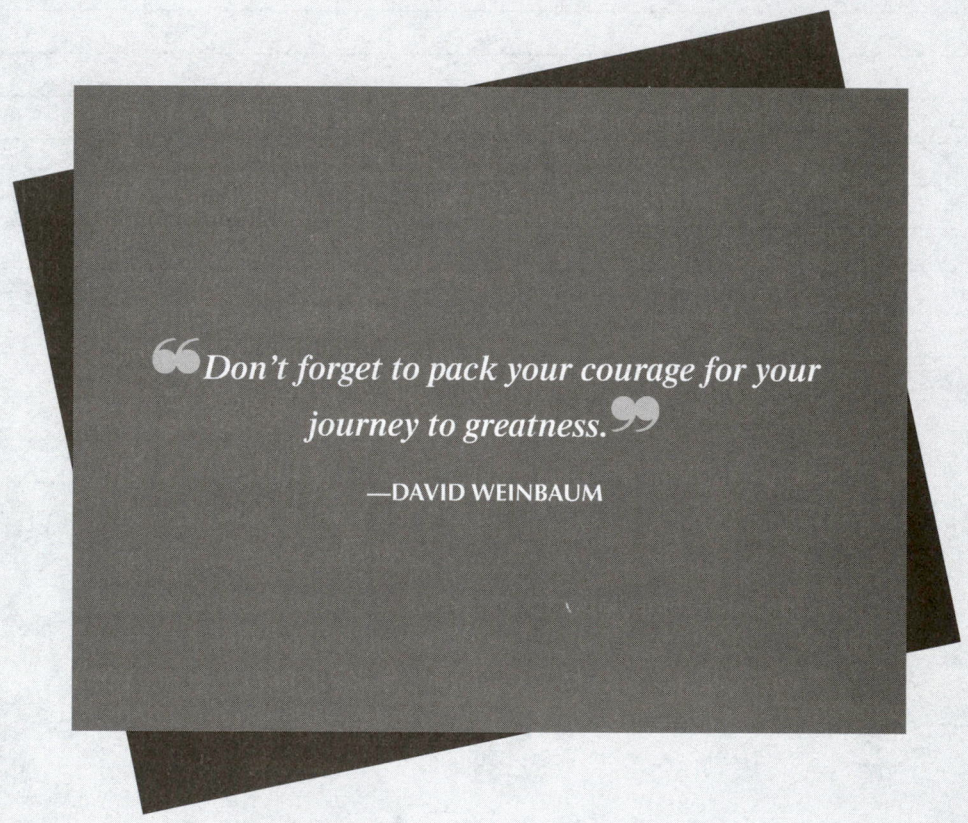

Don't forget to pack your courage for your journey to greatness.

—DAVID WEINBAUM

At last! It's time to wrap it up, pack the portfolio box, and mail it to the National Board for Professional Teaching Standards (NBPTS). For many candidates, finally sending off the box brings out a host of emotions—excitement, anxiety, and exhaustion among them. The goal of this short chapter is to diminish the feelings of angst so you can celebrate that you've accomplished the hugely impressive task of completing your portfolio entries and sending the materials off to NBPTS for scoring. We've provided a Final Checklist (see Figure 6.1) for you to keep track of your progress.

FIGURE 6.1

Final Checklist for Packing and Shipping the Portfolio Box

FINAL CHECKLIST

☐ I know the deadline for mailing the box and if this is the postmark deadline or the due by deadline.

☐ I have made copies of EVERYTHING including portfolio entry (writing), student work samples, DVDs, and forms.

☐ I have checked the NBPTS website for any changes or updates in regards to packing and mailing the box.

☐ I have the General Portfolio Instructions and have read through the step-by-step instructions for assembling, packing, and submitting portfolio entries.

☐ I have printed the Submission at a Glance chart for reference as I pack the box.

☐ I have planned a block of uninterrupted time and have assembled ALL materials following the Assembly Final Inventory Form for each entry.

☐ I have assembled EVERYTHING and re-checked my packing.

☐ I have asked a trusted friend, colleague, or family member to re-check my packing.

☐ I have signed the Attestation Form and Final Inventory Form and placed these in the Forms Envelope.

☐ I have sealed the box following guidelines provided by the NBPTS.

☐ I am ready to mail the box. I have double-checked the mailing address and have determined which mail carrier I will use.

☐ I am requesting a return receipt.

☐ I have checked My Profile on the NBPTS website and determined that my box has been received and that each entry envelope has been acknowledged.

☐ I am celebrating completion of the portfolio and vowing not to second guess my work, nor think about possible scores/results until the score release date!

It is never too soon to plan a schedule for wrapping up the entries and packing the portfolio box. Many candidates aim to complete all portfolio entries a month in advance, as this allows ample time for a final review of the entries, student work samples, and video recordings you plan to submit. Get out your calendar now and count back from the submission deadline. Pay particular attention to *your* submission deadlines because these vary for *Take One!* participants, first-time candidates, retake candidates, and renewal candidates. Also, figure out if the deadlines are *postmark dates* or *received-by dates*. Finally, we strongly advise that you check the NBPTS website for any last-minute updates; sometimes you will find slightly revised instructions or modified submission deadlines.

The portfolio assembly and packing instructions on the CD-ROM can also be found on the NBPTS website. In addition to detailed instructions you will find graphics depicting exactly how you must organize all the materials for each particular entry before mailing the box. Take your time, follow the instructions, and relax. You have invested months of effort and put your heart and soul into this work. Now you're about to bring some measure of closure to the process.

Reviewing and Preparing the Entries for Packing

As a candidate, your intention is to submit portfolio entries that demonstrate in a clear, consistent, and convincing manner how your professional knowledge and skills impact student learning. Although the score your entries receive will not be based on the mechanics of your writing, such as grammar and spelling, you still want to ensure what you submit is relatively free of such errors. The scoring process is positive, rather than negative, so points will not be subtracted from your score for errors. But mechanical errors can sometimes interfere with meaning and distract the reader from the point you're trying to make. In addition, double-check that your documents meet the specifications for font style and size, margins, headers, and so forth. Ask a family member or trusted friend to (re)read your entries with attention paid to mechanics and technical specifications so any glaring errors can be caught and corrected.

You have no doubt spent months and countless hours completing your entries. Prudence dictates that you (re)read the information included in your portfolio instructions, including checking the NBPTS website for any updates to these instructions regarding preparing your entries for submission. Organizing the materials for each portfolio entry following NBPTS guidelines is essential so it will be easier for assessors to access what they need. For example, make sure all of your work is paper clipped and not stapled. And be sure to follow the labeling guidelines so you receive credit for all of your hard work. By the same token, please realize there are no fatal packing errors that would lead NBPTS to *not* score a properly formatted entry that was submitted on time.

When you're done labeling the pieces of your entries, you will likely have extra candidate ID labels left over—don't panic. This is normal since NBPTS provides candidates enough labels for them to correct any errors that might be discovered after affixing a label.

It's always a good idea to ask a family member or close friend to skim through your entries one last time before you pack them up. The intent here is not to read for details, since you've spent more than enough time with these. Rather, you want to be sure everything is in order. For example, maybe your printer skipped a page somehow. Or your page numbering got out of order sometime between your last edit and the printing of the document. You just never know, so it's best to have a second person look over each entry one final time. Someone who has not seen each document multiple times over the last few months is likely to go through the list more slowly and catch any errors you may have overlooked. Use the resource in the portfolio instructions and the Final Checklist (Figure 6.1) before you seal your box.

The last thing to do, before you pack everything up, is *make a copy of all of your materials* (including videos and student work samples). This is for two reasons. First, in the event the package does not make it to NBPTS (or is damaged beyond recognition en route), you will be able to quickly send another copy. Second, looking ahead optimistically to when you are considering certificate renewal, it may be helpful to review your original portfolio entries; store your copy in a safe, secure place. Please keep in mind, though, that your portfolio represents an assessment document that, once submitted, is confidential. Sharing with others, particularly with National Board candidates, is a violation of NBPTS guidelines and could result in the voiding of your scores.

But what happens if you're not done with all of the portfolio entries by the deadline? Despite all of your forward planning and best intentions, you may find yourself still writing on the day all materials must be sent off. First of all, don't panic. You're a professional and you need to be pragmatic about this situation. If you find yourself with an incomplete or missing entry, by all means *mail in what you have*. Every entry you submit will be scored, but you will not receive an overall candidate score if fewer than four portfolio entries (and six assessment center exercises) are submitted. If you are a first-time candidate, the scores on the entries you submitted on time will be banked for up to two more candidate cycles. You can then apply to become a retake candidate (and pay the required fees) to submit the other entries. See the section in Chapter 8 titled "What Is Retake Candidacy?" for additional information.

Packing and Shipping the Portfolio Box

⚠ First, a word of caution: We strongly recommend you pack your portfolio box individually or with a trusted friend who can double-check things rather than participating in a candidate "packing party" where there is the potential for mislabeling or mixing up your materials with those of other candidates. Not that it would happen to *you*, but better safe than sorry. However, if you feel it would be personally meaningful to participate in a packing party, please take steps to safeguard against the comingling of documents. We know it is fun to take this last step (of the portfolio process) together, but want you to do so carefully.

One pitfall to watch for is mislabeling or mixing up your DVDs. Play each of them before you affix the labels provided by NBPTS. This is a nice opportunity to see yourself in action one more time and appreciate the journey you've been through to this point. After you've checked this, double-check when packing the DVDs that each is matched to the correct entry and placed inside the corresponding envelope.

When it comes time to seal the box, refer to the NBPTS instructions for information on what kind of tape is preferred. Affix a sticky note with the mailing address to the front of the box and double-check that it's not changed by going to the NBPTS website or calling 1-800-22TEACH. Now you're ready to send the portfolio off to be scored.

You can mail the portfolio box via the U.S. Postal Service or any delivery company of your choosing. What is most important, however, is to plan ahead and be certain you know the company's pickup and delivery schedules and timelines. As the story in the accompanying sidebar conveys, you might also consider whether you need a keepsake photo of your box as it leaves your hands. Remember to request a return receipt and use it

❝After months and months of writing and rewriting my four entries, I was smiling all the way as I went to mail off the completed portfolio. Suddenly, as I walked into the postal store, I felt like a parent who was about to let my child go off to kindergarten for the first time. I just didn't want to let go no matter how relieved I was in having finished the entries. Fear rushed over me as an image of my entries getting lost in delivery flashed through my mind. Nonetheless, the more rational part of me compromised with that fear and led me to let go of the portfolio as long as I had a keepsake of the moment. I took out my camera phone and snapped not one but several pictures of me handing over the entries and their being processed for shipment. With this photographic evidence at least I could feel some relief in knowing I had proof that I mailed the entries. In the end, while it turned out such proof was a bit overdramatic, it sure was fun to upload the pictures to share the moment with the world as I left my entries in the good hands of the delivery folks! ❞

—NBCT, MIDDLE CHILDHOOD GENERALIST

to verify that your box has reached its destination by checking with the shipping company. Once this has been confirmed, log in to the NBPTS website and go to My Profile to check that each entry envelope has been received and processed.

Once you have mailed the box, celebrate your submission as an accomplishment! Set aside any anxieties, and try not to second-guess your work or stress about your score or achievement of National Board Certification®. In early November, begin checking the NBPTS website periodically for news about score release, which occurs by December 31 (but typically happens sooner).

If you have not yet completed the assessment center exercises, it is now time to devote your attention to preparing yourself for your scheduled assessment session. Chapter 7 provides ideas that will help you with this process.

MY THOUGHTS

(Use this space to record ideas generated from reading this chapter.)

_____

_____

_____

_____

_____

_____

_____

_____

_____

_____

_____

_____

_____

_____

_____

_____

_____

_____

Preparing for the Assessment Center

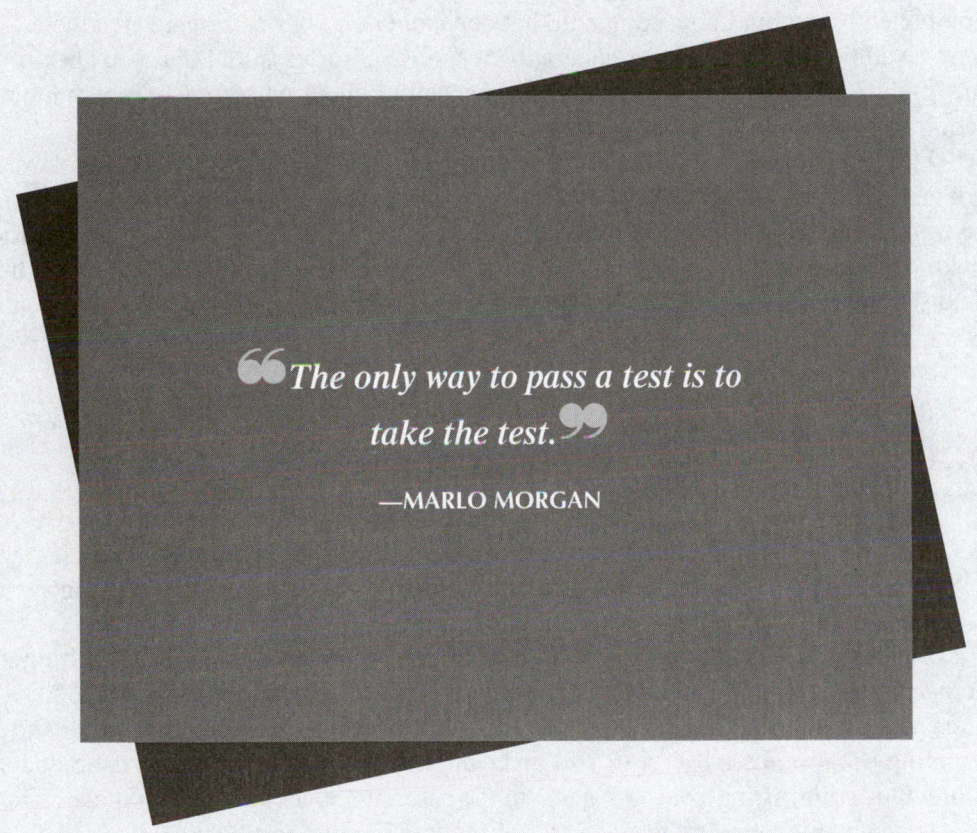

The second portion of the National Board process is the assessment center. This portion is designed to assess the depth and breadth of your content knowledge as well as your pedagogical content knowledge (including developmentally appropriate practices and strategies). In this chapter, we will provide a brief overview of the assessment center, describe some tips on how to study for the assessment center exercises, and give a brief description of what you can expect at your assessment center session.

What Are the Assessment Center Exercises?

As mentioned in Chapter 1, the assessment center exercises are six constructed-response items that are designed to test how well you know the content of your certificate area and in many cases how well you know how to teach that content. Each exercise addresses an area deemed important by the National Board for that certificate area and developmental range. Some exercise prompts are strictly about content, and others may combine content and pedagogy. While there are only six exercises, each exercise may have multiple prompts. You will have 30 minutes to complete your response for each of the six exercises. Because the assessment center exercises are done at a formal testing center under contract with NBPTS, your responses will be completed on-site. Your responses to most exercises will be completed by typing into a computer, but depending on your certificate area there may be additional methods for generating responses. It is essential that you check the instructions for your certificate area for specifics about what may or may not be required or allowed when completing the exercises.

The content theme or focus of the six exercises you will have to respond to are not a secret! The descriptions of these as well as the scoring guidelines for each can be found in the assessment center section of the NBPTS website. As with the portfolio, the website should be your first step for preparing for the assessment center. The next section provides some tips on how to get ready for this part of the certification process.

Organizing for the Assessment Center

As John Wooden said, "Failing to prepare is preparing to fail." So, it is important to start looking into what will be required of you in the assessment center. Many candidates perceive the portfolio entries as being more challenging and mattering more since these account for 60 percent of your score and have greater writing demands than the assessment center exercises. However, it would be a mistake to presume that the assessment center does not require commensurate preparation and planning because these exercises still make up 40 percent of your overall candidate score. Our point: Bring your "A" game to the assessment center. You can make your assessment center appointment as early as January in your certification cycle (but only once all your fees are paid).

Here are some tips to start the process:

1. *Download your materials.* If you have not already done so, go to the NBPTS website and download the Assessment Center Policies and Guidelines document as well as the Assessment at a Glance document for your certificate. The Policies and Guidelines document details specific instructions for making and rescheduling appointments as well as what you can expect at the testing center. The Assessment at a Glance document contains an overview of the six assessment center exercises for your certificate area. For each exercise there is a description of the focus of each exercise (for example, it could be addressing student difficulties with making sense of inferential statistics for math, responding to a scenario involving a struggling reader, or analyzing graphical representations of data for science). There are also some retired, previously used

assessment center prompts to use for practice; we'll discuss these later. Next, go to the scoring section of the NBPTS website and download the Scoring Guide for your certificate area. Part I of the guide has general information about scoring, while Part II has specific scoring criteria for your certificate, including the scoring rubric used for each assessment center exercise.

2. *Organize and analyze your materials.* Some suggestions to organize your materials include making a binder, with one tab for each assessment center exercise; creating a digital folder for each exercise; or creating a wiki to keep all your directions and study resources together. Once you have an organizational system in place, collect as much as you can; when it comes time to focus on studying you'll have plenty to draw from. Read the Assessment at a Glance and Scoring Guide materials *for each exercise*. As you do so, think about the following:

   - What are the standards addressed, and what are some critical phrases or ideas from these standards that would be useful to include in your responses?

   - What are assessors looking for in your responses? What type of knowledge is being assessed? Are there specific terms, theories, or strategies you will be expected to know? What are some key phrases from the Scoring Guide that you need to keep in mind? Think about what the exercise is asking you to demonstrate and how your response can provide clear, consistent, and convincing evidence of the standards.

   - Knowing what you know about the standards and Scoring Guide, can you come up with some possible questions; like we often advise our school-aged students, put yourself in the shoes of the assessor for a moment and think, "If this were my test, what questions would I ask?"

   - What sort of studying do you need to do? For example, if you will be asked about geometry, but haven't taught it in a while, you may want to review a textbook and talk to a colleague who teaches geometry. Pay particular attention to the age range for students in your certificate area. If you have been teaching third grade for the last several years and are not so familiar with the developmental issues facing kindergarteners, you may need to consult a child development textbook or talk to a kindergarten teacher.

   - Finally, if the exercise asks about a particular instructional strategy, like the use of technology or manipulatives, brainstorm lessons you can reference in your response.

The Assessment Center Planning Organizer (Figure 7.1) may help you organize this work. We encourage you to complete one of these for each assessment center exercise and include them in your assessment center binder or file. You can review these notes immediately prior to going into the assessment center (but be aware you cannot bring them with you or use them during the actual appointment).

3. *Take a practice test.* There are two retired, released prompts for each certificate area in the Assessment at a Glance document available from the NBPTS website. Consider printing these and devoting an hour (30 minutes each) to typing responses to the two exercises back-to-back to simulate what it will be like in the assessment center. Make it as real as possible—minimize distractions and don't look at your notes. After writing your responses to the practice prompts, use the Scoring Guide rubric criteria to evaluate your responses. This is a great activity to do with a colleague or in a group if you have access to other candidates. Reflect on this experience and think about what it tells you. Do you

FIGURE 7.1

Assessment Center Planning Organizer

Title of exercise:

Description of exercise:

Standards addressed by the exercise and key phrases that may be helpful	
Key phrases from Scoring Guide	
Study resources for this exercise	
Possible questions I may be asked	
Possible units, lessons, or content themes that apply to this exercise	

Copyright © Pearson Education

need to brush up on some content topics or pedagogical terminology? Do you need more timed writing practice? Make a plan to address these needs. If you're looking for more practice after going through the released prompts and analyzing how you did, we recommend a quick Internet search for "assessment center prompts" to turn up additional resources.

4. *Go through the NBPTS assessment tutorial.* On the NBPTS website's assessment center page, there is a link to a free tutorial for the computer interface you will use for the actual assessment center exercises. Download the tutorial and use it to get comfortable with using this to type responses.

5. *Make your assessment center appointment at the earliest possible opportunity.* Just like making a dinner reservation at a popular restaurant, the longer you wait, the fewer choices you'll have. Plus, getting it on your calendar may be motivating. Some candidates prefer to tackle the assessment center early, even before the portfolio submission deadline; others prefer to wait until after portfolio submission. There is no "right" or "wrong" way—make the choice that best suits your work style. We recommend, though, you make time to complete the analysis as previously suggested in #3 before you make your appointment so you can take into account the amount of preparation time you will need. For instance, if you know based on your analysis that you need to spend time talking with other teachers or reviewing content, you may want to make your appointment later rather than sooner. The take-home message here is to make a good choice about your assessment center appointment considering your work style, preparation needs, and availability.

6. *Make special accommodations ahead of time.* If you require any special accommodations, download the Request for Testing Accommodations document from **www.nbpts.org**. It details what accommodations can be made, what documentation is required, contact information, and submission deadlines.

Resources for Studying for the Assessment Center Exercises

Abundant resources are available to help you prepare for your assessment center exercises. Several are listed in the Assessment at a Glance document and the Policies and Guidelines document provided by NBPTS. Here are some others we have found useful:

- State content standards/framework and Common Core State Standards documents may provide good explanations of grade-level and course-specific content. What is most useful to you is the rationale and explanation of the standards, not simply the list of the standards themselves. Read through these, especially for the grades or specific topics you do not normally teach. If something sounds confusing or really unfamiliar, tag that for further study.

- Using content textbooks can also be helpful. Start by reading the chapter summaries, especially for content you typically do not teach. If you have a difficult time understanding the topic just by reading the summary, it would probably be a good idea to read that chapter carefully.

- For generalist certificate candidates, the book *Yardsticks: Children in the Classroom Ages 4–14: A Resource for Parents and Teachers* by Chip Wood (2007) is a good tool to give a longitudinal perspective on children's development (cognitive, behavioral, motor, and social) to help you think about how this relates to your support of student learning.

- The "for Dummies" line of books, such as *Statistics for Dummies* or *Biology for Dummies*, may be helpful once you've identified a specific content area for review. Many of these titles are available at your local library.

- Web-based materials are abundant. A couple of sites we recommend you search for content-specific resources are **www.teachertube.com** and **www.learner. org**. Each of these has valuable tutorials on specific content and is designed for teachers and students alike. In addition, be sure to visit the websites of professional organizations relevant to your certificate area (e.g., National Council of Teachers of English; National Council of Teachers of Mathematics; National Association for the Education of Young Children).

Test Day Tips

When test day arrives, there are some things you can do to make sure you are at your best:

1. Get plenty of rest. OK, so this technically is something you do the night *before* test day, but it is important!
2. Eat prior to the appointment and bring snacks (like raisins or a granola bar) to eat during your scheduled break to keep up your energy. Brain cells run on glucose, so keep them happy. Candidates will be allowed to take a 15-minute break after completing three entries. Use it or lose it. A break taken at any other point during the session will be taken out of your testing time.

3. Be on time. Plan to arrive 30 minutes prior to your appointment time to complete the check-in procedures. If you are more than 30 minutes late for your appointment, you may lose active candidacy status and must pay a reinstatement fee before being allowed to schedule another appointment. If you are worried at all about this, consider a test run—drive to your testing center site a week ahead of your scheduled date so it will be somewhat familiar to you when you go on test day.

4. Be aware of what you need to bring to your appointment. Each certificate has different requirements, so read the Assessment Center Policies and Guidelines document carefully. Some candidates must bring in some candidate ID labels—are you one of them? *All* candidates must bring government-issued photo identification—plan for this like you would for airport security (though the testing center allows liquids and won't make you take off your shoes). You will not be permitted to take the test without proper photo identification. If you're unsure about this requirement, call 1-800-22TEACH (1-800-228-3224) or check the policies and guidelines document to make sure your photo ID is acceptable.

5. Each assessment center session begins with completing a nondisclosure agreement and a brief tutorial. Use the tutorial time to familiarize yourself with the tools, like cutting and pasting text and turning the timer on and off. Most candidates are rather anxious when they first sit down. The tutorial is not timed, so if you can, use these first few moments to get used to the room and the situation. Take a few breaths before starting your entry.

6. Be aware of what you *won't* be able to bring in (writing utensils, coats, hats, purse, etc.). Some exceptions are so-called minor comfort aids such as cough drops, eyeglasses, and earplugs. Reread the Assessment Center Policy and Guidelines if you are unsure about an item. Most centers have lockers to secure personal items during testing, but call your testing site if you have any questions.

> **❝***On test day, I just threw on some comfy clothes and put on a hat and went out the door. I didn't realize I couldn't wear a hat in the testing room! It seems silly, but the fact that my "hat hair" was being captured on camera was really distracting.***❞**
>
> —NBCT, ADOLESCENCE AND YOUNG ADULTHOOD SCIENCE

Strategies for Attacking the Test

Here are some final strategies that will help you do your best on the exercises. We encourage you to rehearse these during your practice tests.

1. Be mindful of your pacing. Most questions consist of multiple parts. Each section is timed for 30 minutes; therefore, if there are three scoring criteria, there will most likely be three subsections. This would give you approximately 8 minutes for each subsection and 6 minutes to read and think about the prompts. Have a time-keeping device and use it when practicing for the exercises so you become accustomed, for example, to what 8 minutes feels like.

2. To make sure you address each part of each exercise, start off by writing a topic sentence or short answer to each subsection. Then go back and write more thorough responses. This way, in case you don't complete your response in time, you will at least give the assessors a chance to know your main ideas for each. It is important to know that points are not awarded for each subsection

> **"I was really anxious about the Assessment Center. All the practice I did paid off because I was familiar with the test format, so I knew there would be multiple parts to the questions and had a sense of how much time I could devote to each part. Once it started, I knew I could do this."**
>
> —NBCT, EARLY CHILDHOOD GENERALIST

and averaged to get the total exercise score; rather, each exercise is scored holistically, with one score given for the entire set of responses. That being said, your score will be negatively affected by a blank section. Don't miss an opportunity to provide clear, consistent, and convincing evidence of your knowledge.

3. After you've written a strong topic sentence, feel free to use bullets, outlines, or lists as well as sentences to start your responses. After you've sketched out some ideas, go back and rewrite them using complete sentences. Keep in mind the assessment center is not a writing test. It is a test to see what you know about a specific set of content and pedagogical standards. Do not worry about artful transitions, clever analogies, or even proper spelling or punctuation. Using bullets or short phrases to make your points clear is acceptable, So long as writing errors do not impede the assessor's ability to understand your ideas, you are fine.

A Word About Test Anxiety

Test anxiety, as a concept, has been around since the 1950s. It is defined as an unpleasant feeling or emotional state in reference to a test situation (Schunk, Pintrich, & Meece, 2008). This usually contributes to poor performance. There are two components to test anxiety: a cognitive component and an emotional component. Cognitive worry usually has to do with the negative thoughts that run through a test taker's head during the exam such as, "I'm going to run out of time," "I can't remember the answer," or "I'm going to fail and then I won't certify." The emotional component refers to the feelings one experiences as a result of anxiety such as fear, nausea, or unease.

Different strategies can help alleviate each of these components. Familiarity with the content and format of exams reduces test anxiety, so take the time to review the assessment center materials and take one or more practice tests. Start studying and practicing well in advance of your test date. Setting aside just 30 to 60 minutes a week for a few weeks can really help. Learning to pace your responses, as described, will help alleviate the concern about running out of time. Finally, think positively. This assessment is about the knowledge and skills that are the basis for what you do every day! Pretend you are answering a question asked of you by a novice teacher when you respond to the assessment center prompts. It is entirely likely that you respond to questions of a similar nature all the time when talking with colleagues or maybe even in a more formal setting as an instructional coach or mentor. Approach the prompts as you would with a colleague and it may be more comfortable.

Finally, don't think about whether you will certify. Earning certification is a wonderful recognition, but what is even more valuable is the professional growth you experienced by taking part in the certification process. Few teachers even attempt to do what you are doing. Regardless of your scores, you took a risk and are likely a better teacher for it.

After you ship your portfolio entries and complete the assessment center exercises, the long wait begins. Chapter 8 describes what you can expect back from NBPTS on score release day.

Additional Resources

Although the process of certification is about what you know and are able to do, candidates find it helpful to prepare for the assessment center exercises by brushing up on content area knowledge and skills, in addition to pedagogy for the early and middle childhood candidates. Following are a number of Web-based resources and professional resources that may prove helpful. Please note that these are not necessarily resources the authors are endorsing, but rather ones we have found helpful or that candidates have recommended as useful.

Web-Based Resources

- California Learning Resource Network digital textbooks (**www.clrn.org/fdti**)
- CK12 "flexbook" open source, customizable textbooks (**www.ck12.org**)
- International Society for Technology in Education (**www.iste.org**)
- Directory of free online textbooks (**www.textbookrevolution.org**)
- International Reading Association (**www.reading.org**)
- National Association for Bilingual Education (**www.nabe.org**)
- National Association for Health and Physical Education (**www.aahperd.org/naspe**)
- National Association for the Education of Young Children (**www.naeyc.org**)
- National Council for History Education (**www.history.org/nche**)
- National Council for Teachers of English (**www.ncte.org**)
- National Council of Teachers of Mathematics (**www.nctm.org**)
- National Council for the Social Studies (**www.ncss.org**)
- National Science Teachers Association (**www.nsta.org**)
- Teachers of English to Speakers of Other Languages (**www.tesol.org**)
- Wikibooks open content textbook collection (**en.wikibooks.org**)

Resource Books by Content Area or Instructional Topic

Reading, Language Arts, Literacy Development

Cunningham, P. M. (2010). *Classrooms that work: They can all read and write,* 5th ed. Columbus, OH: Allyn & Bacon/Pearson.

Harvey, S., & Goudvis, A. (2007). *Strategies that work: Teaching comprehension for understanding and engagement.* Portland, ME: Stenhouse.

Keene, E. O., & Zimmermann, S. (2007). *Mosaic of thought: The power of comprehension strategy instruction.* Portsmouth, ME: Heinemann.

Miller, D. (2002). *Reading with meaning: Teaching comprehension in the primary grades.* Portland, ME: Stenhouse.

National Institute for Literacy. (2003) *Put reading first: The research building blocks for teaching children to read.* Retrieved from **http://www .nifl.gov**

Routman, R. (2005). *Writing essentials: Raising expectations and results while simplifying teaching.* Portsmouth, ME: Heinemann.

Mathematics

Donovan, M. S., & Bransford, J. D. (Eds.). (2005). *How students learn: Mathematics in the classroom.* Washington, DC: National Academies Press.

Dudgeon, J. (2005). *Children's errors in mathematics: Understanding common misconceptions.* Exeter, UK: Learning Matters.

National Council of Teachers of Mathematics. (2011). *Achieving fluency: Special education and mathematics.* Reston, VA: Author.

National Council of Teachers of Mathematics. (2007). *Mathematics teaching today: Improving practice, improving student learning.* Reston, VA: Author.

National Council of Teachers of Mathematics. *Curriculum Focal Points* series for grades preK-8. **http://www.nctm.org/catalog/product. aspx?ID=13615**

National Council of Teachers of Mathematics. *Essential understanding* series for grades preK-12. **http://www.nctm.org/catalog/productsview.aspx?id=129**

Ryan, J., & Williams, J. (2007) *Children's mathematics 4–15: Learning from errors and misconceptions.* Maidenhead, UK: Open University Press, McGraw-Hill Education.

Science

Bell, R. (2007). *Teaching the nature of science through process skills: Activities for grades 3–8.* Columbus, OH: Allyn & Bacon.

Donovan, M. S., & Bransford, J. D. (Eds.). (2005). *How students learn: Science in the classroom.* Washington, DC: National Academies Press.

Llewellyn, D. (2004). *Teaching high school science through inquiry: A case study approach.* Thousand Oaks, CA: Corwin Press.

Llewellyn, D. (2007). *Inquire within: Implementing inquiry-based science standards in grades 3–8.* Thousand Oaks, CA: Corwin Press.

Olson, S., & Loucks-Horsley (Eds.). (2000). Inquiry and the National Science Education Standards: A guide for teaching and learning. Washington, DC: National Academies Press.

Health and Physical Education

American Cancer Society. (2007). *National health education standards* (2nd ed.). Athens, GA: Joint Committee on National Health Education Standards.

National Association for Sport and Physical Education (2nd ed.). (2004). *Moving into the future: National standards for physical education.* Reston, VA: Author.

Social Studies

Donovan, M.S., & Bransford, J. D. (Eds.). (2005). *How students learn: History in the classroom.* Washington, DC: National Academies Press.

Fritzer, P. J. and Brewer, E. A. (2009). *Social studies content for elementary and middle school teachers*, 2nd ed. Boston, MA: Allyn & Bacon.

Zinn, H. (2003). *A people's history of the United States: 1492—present.* New York: HarperCollins.

Special Education, Inclusion, and Response to Intervention

Fitzell, S. (2011). *RTI strategies for secondary teachers.* Thousand Oaks, CA: Corwin Press.

Friend, M. (2010). Special education: Contemporary perspectives for school professionals. Upper Saddle River, NJ: Prentice Hall.

Howard, M. (2009). *RTI from all sides: What every teacher needs to know.* Portsmouth, NH: Heinemann.

Werts, M., Culatta, R., & Tompkins, J. (2007). *Fundamentals of special education: What every teacher needs to know.* New York: Merrill.

Parent and Community Partnerships

Canter, L. (2001). *Parents on your side: A teacher's guide to creating positive relationships with parents,* 2nd ed. Bloomington, IN: Solution Tree.

Power, B. (1999). *Parent power: Energizing home–school communication.* Portsmouth, ME: Heinemann.

Children's Play

Heidemann, S., & Hewitt, D. (2009). *Play: The pathway from theory to practice.* St. Paul, MN: Redleaf Press.

Graves, D. H. (2006). *A sea of faces: The importance of knowing your students.* Portsmouth, ME: Heinemann.

Guillaume, A., Yopp, R. H., & Yopp, H. K. (2007). *50 strategies for active teaching: Engaging K–12 learners in the classroom.* Columbus, OH: Pearson.

Wood, C. (2007). *Yardsticks: Children in the classroom ages 4–14: A resource for parents and teachers.* Greenfield, MA: Northeast Foundation for Children.

MY THOUGHTS

(Use this space to record ideas generated from reading this chapter, including topics you plan to review for the assessment center and reflections on test anxiety.)

_____

_____

_____

_____

_____

_____

_____

_____

_____

_____

_____

_____

_____

_____

_____

_____

_____

_____

_____

8

Planning for Score Release

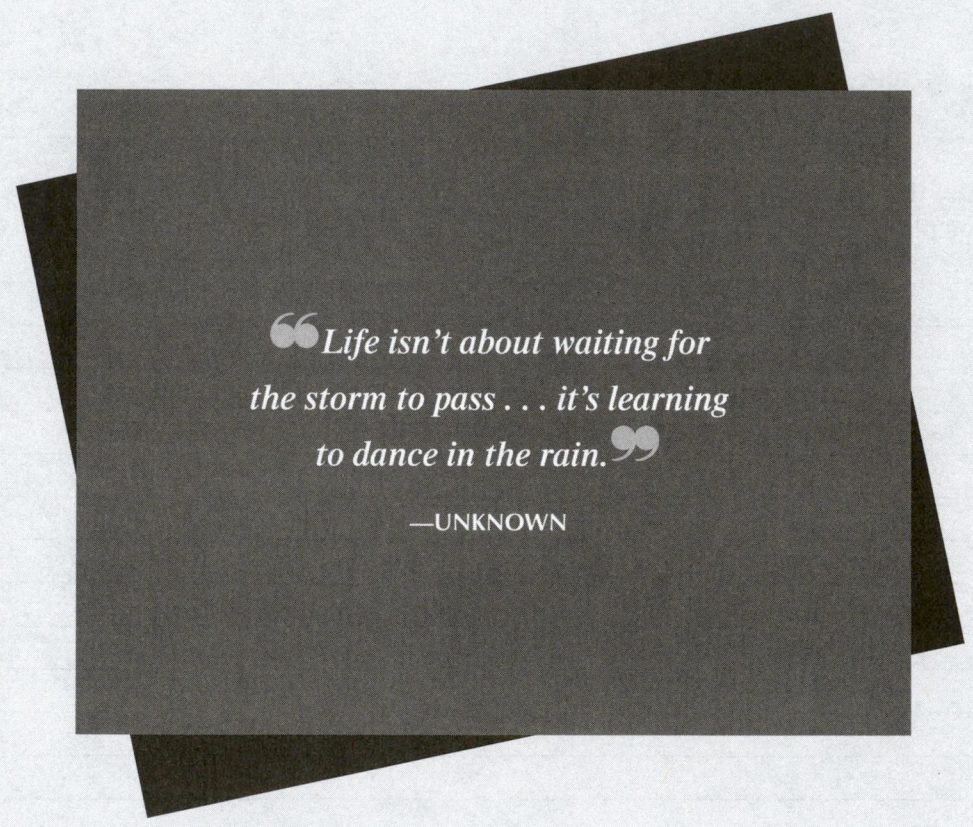

> ❝*Life isn't about waiting for the storm to pass . . . it's learning to dance in the rain.*❞
>
> —UNKNOWN

No doubt that once you have submitted your portfolio entries and completed the assessment center exercises, you'll feel as though you have just weathered a storm! Again, as noted in an earlier chapter, simply completing the process is reason to celebrate. Once scores are released it will be your time to dance in the rain; whether you achieve certification or not, you are to be commended for your journey.

In this chapter we will start with some facts about scores and scoring meant to dispel some common myths you might hear. Then we'll review how your total score is calculated using the raw scores from the four entries and six exercises. Last, but by no means least, we will take time to discuss retake (sometimes referred to as "advanced") candidacy for those who might not yet have achieved certification. We are huge believers in the National Board Certification process as not only a measure of high-impact teaching but also as a transformative experience in our professional lives. The option of retake candidacy acknowledges that this journey may require additional time to reflect on and refine one's practices; to augment one's content and pedagogical knowledge; and to learn to identify and describe clear, convincing, and consistent evidence of one's existing practices in order to meet what have been acknowledged as the highest standards within the education profession.

Just the Facts: Addressing Myths About Scoring

In our many years working with candidates, we've heard just about everything. Perhaps due to the high-stakes nature of this assessment and the rather comprehensive scoring process, there are some persistent myths that we hear. Rather than list these and potentially add to their longevity, we'll give you their related facts so you can clear things up for yourself and others.

> **Fact #1:** First and foremost, scores are released only to you as a candidate and are for your eyes only.

Only the candidate can access the score report through My Profile, and only the candidate can input the candidate ID number along with additional verification data, typically birthdate and social security number. This is yet another reason why as a candidate you have been continually cautioned to keep close tabs on your candidate ID number. From our perspective, there is *never* a reason to share your scores except in the case that you are working with a trained candidate support provider as a retake candidate to retake portions of the assessment. Achieving certification is proof enough of your status as an accomplished teacher—keep the scores to yourself.

> **Fact #2:** Scores are released to candidates on or before December 31 of the year in which your portfolio entries and assessment center exercises were due and completed.

Although scores are often released sooner (even as early as mid-November), do not expect scores before December 31unless you receive notification from NBPTS about an earlier date.

> **Fact #3:** The names of educators who have achieved certification are made public on NBPTS Certification Day, which usually occurs approximately two weeks after scores have been released to candidates.

Again, no scores are released, only the names of those who have achieved certification. Names of those not yet achieving certification are never made public. The journey toward certification is a personal one, and NBPTS does its part to keep it that way.

Fact #4: Score reports may be accessed by candidates online only and
are no longer mailed to candidates.

If you try to log in to view yours on the first day scores are released, remember, there are thousands of other candidates in waiting (CIWs) trying to access their score reports, too. Go online early because you may need to make several attempts to access your scores.

Understanding Your Score Report

Once you access your score report you will see a raw exercise score (RES) and weighting factor (W) for each portfolio entry and each assessment center exercise. Each raw entry score is multiplied by the weighting factor (RES × W) to determine the scaled score (SS) for each component. For statistical purposes, a uniform constant of 12 points is added to the sum total of your scaled scores to determine your total weighted score (TWS).

The magic number is 275. You need a total weighted score of 275 to achieve certification. Another myth dispelled. Yes, you can achieve certification without having earned a passing score on every portfolio entry or assessment center exercise. Candidates are sometimes disappointed to receive less than perfect scores or to achieve certification with exactly the 275 points needed. However, there is no need to feel disheartened. As long as your score is 275 or higher, you are an NBCT. If there is a specific entry or exercise for which your score was not as strong, think about this as an area for continued growth—perhaps this will be something to comment on when you work on your Profile of Professional Growth eight or nine years from now as part of the certificate renewal process.

What Is Retake Candidacy?

If your score report indicates that you did not certify, take a deep breath and be prepared to stay on course to achieve National Board Certification® as a retake candidate. NBPTS understands that it may take more than one candidate cycle for you to achieve certification. You are permitted to go through a total of three cycles as you work to show clear, consistent, and convincing evidence that your professional practice and its impact on students as well as your content and pedagogical knowledge reflect the standards set by the organization. Note that raw scores of 2.75 or higher from your first attempt at certification are valid only for the next two candidate cycles. If you've not done so already, be sure to go through the section in the Preface titled, "How to Use This Book: Retake or Advanced Candidate." There we direct you to the parts of this book most helpful to retake candidates, including some important tips and reminders for you to consider.

Remember that this should be thought of as a professional journey that sometimes takes one year, sometimes two or three. It is not uncommon for candidates to take longer than a one-year journey, as the certification rate is not 100 percent.

Candidates have shared that, whether they achieve certification or not, they have become better educators as a result of participating in this rigorous process.

There are any number of reasons why a candidate may not achieve certification on the first attempt or perhaps the second attempt. We know it's not easy to move into retake candidate status and respect your decision about this. This process begins by first believing that you can do this because you *are* an accomplished teacher. However, to earn certification you must determine what you will do differently this time so that through the lens of your certificate standards you describe, analyze, and reflect on what you know and are able to do to impact student learning and achievement using clear, consistent, and convincing evidence.

Once you have had a chance to thoroughly review your score report and have given yourself a bit of time to consider what you'll do differently, it is time to take action. Along with the tips for getting started given in Chapter 3, the following steps will help as you continue your journey.

Determining What to Retake

The most important decision you must make before applying as a retake candidate is what portfolio entries and/or assessment center exercises you will retake. Some aspects of this decision are easy—for example, you cannot retake any entry or exercise for which you received a raw score of 2.75 or higher. Also, the National Board will always use your highest score, not the most recent score, for any entry or exercise that you've submitted more than once. Before reading on, use the Score Analysis Worksheet (Table 8.1) to help with the initial process of identifying your potential for earning additional points. You might also explore the retake calculator tool on the NBPTS website that allows you to figure out how many points you could gain if you were to retake various combinations of entries and exercises.

TABLE 8.1 Score Analysis Worksheet

Entry or Exercise	Eligible for Retake? (Raw Score < 2.75)	Maximum Possible Score (4.25) − Current Raw Score (RES) = Potential Gain (PG)	Weighting Factor (W)	PG × W = Maximum Possible Score Gain
Entry 1				
Entry 2				
Entry 3				
Entry 4				
Exercise 1				
Exercise 2				
Exercise 3				
Exercise 4				
Exercise 5				
Exercise 6				

Now it's time to strategize. Using your knowledge of the potential score gain and knowing your strengths as well as areas for growth, you want to put together a game plan that includes not only which entries and exercises you will retake but also what you will do to aim for an improved outcome. Keep in mind that while a lower raw score means more room for improvement, the actual outcome of your retake efforts depends greatly on your ability to determine what you need to do to improve your score. NBPTS has given you some ideas to start with. For each portfolio entry and assessment center exercise with a raw score of less than 3.74, your score report will include standardized feedback comments that are specific to your certificate area, standards, and scoring rubric. Read these carefully and take them into consideration when exploring your retake options. In addition, think through your responses to the following questions, either individually or together with a support provider, to further inform your decision making about retake options. You will likely have some *a-ha* moments as you do this.

- Am I more comfortable retaking portfolio entries or assessment center exercises? Should I attempt only one or the other or, if I have the option, should I retake both portfolio entries and assessment center exercises?

- How much time do I have to devote to my retake candidacy efforts? Keep in mind this will be a far less daunting task than your initial journey as you have some prior experience with it and will be completing fewer entries and/or exercises.

- What are my own personal strengths and weaknesses as a candidate? For example, if I am pursuing a generalist certificate, where do my strengths lie in the content areas? Am I more likely to achieve certification if I retake the math assessment center exercise rather than the literacy exercise?

- Think about the work that was submitted in relationship to the scoring guide for each entry, the scores received, and the feedback provided. To what degree did the entry I submitted meet the requirements? What might I do differently if I were to retake an entry (different in terms of planning lessons, my instructional strategies, video recording, student work samples, my analysis and reflection, etc.)?

- What are my strengths and weaknesses with describing, analyzing, and reflecting evidence of the impact of my practice on student learning? Was I clear, consistent, and convincing? How well did the evidence I presented characterize what a high-impact teacher should know and be able to do, based on my certificate standards?

⚠ Once you've responded to these prompts, make your decision about retake entries and exercises based on a combination of the points you need to achieve certification and your awareness of your strengths and areas for growth. A word of caution—you do not want to put all your eggs in one basket. It is advisable to err on the side of caution and plan to retake enough entries and/or exercises to earn *more than* the 275 minimum needed to achieve certification. After making your selection, hurry up and apply as a retake candidate as the deadline to do so is typically in late January following score release. Check the NBPTS for the exact deadline for your candidate cycle. The next section will offer some support in getting yourself back into the candidate groove.

Jumping into the Retake Entries and/or Exercises

Congratulations! You've cleared the first few hurdles as a retake candidate—deciding which portfolio entries and/or assessment center exercises make the most sense for you to work on again and getting yourself registered. You're off to a good start. We want to offer some targeted ideas for the work that will be required so you have a strong finish as well.

1. Reexamine the instructions for each portfolio entry you will retake. Make note of any instructions and requirements to which you want to pay extra attention as you put together your retake entries.

2. Reexamine the standards being assessed in each entry you will retake. Make note of specific standards for which you plan to provide stronger evidence.

3. Reexamine the scoring guide and evaluation of evidence guide for each entry and exercise you will retake. Think about how your retake entries and/or exercises will demonstrate the evidence required and make note of particular areas you will focus on improving.

4. If you received a 2.75 or higher raw score for an entry, reread this as a way to remind yourself that you have what it takes to achieve certification and to look for strengths in how you put the entry together that you will apply to your retake work.

5. After having analyzed your previous portfolio entries, it is time to start fresh. Read about and make note of the format specifications for each portfolio entry you will retake. Be sure to use the "Entry Planning" section of Chapter 3, including the Entry Planning Worksheet (Table 3.1).

6. Use Chapters 4 and 5 of this book to help you refine the ways you select, analyze, and reflect on evidence through your written entries.

7. If you are retaking portfolio Entry 4, check with NBPTS by phone or through the online help service about what you may and may not reuse in terms of previously documented accomplishments. Use the "Documented Accomplishments Entry" section of Chapter 5 to help focus your search for and description of accomplishments and evidence of their impact on student learning. The Documented Accomplishments Categories Chart in the NBPTS portfolio instructions may also be useful.

8. Review the tips in Chapter 6 if you will be packaging portfolio entries to send off to NBPTS with student work samples and/or video recordings.

9. If you are retaking an assessment center exercise, reread the description and standards assessed and use Chapter 7 to further direct your preparation efforts.

Closing Thoughts for Retake Candidates

We know how hard you have worked to reach this point as a professional. Do what you can to capitalize on this opportunity to examine your practice against the rigor of the NBPTS standards and of the certification process. Remember, too, that the success rate does increase with the second and third attempts. Keep your head up and your mind focused on the goal at hand—achieving National Board Certification. We know you can do it! You are an accomplished teacher and you do impact students in powerful ways each and every day. Now articulate that through clear, convincing, and consistent evidence as you continue your journey toward National Board Certification!

MY THOUGHTS

(Use this space to record ideas generated from reading this chapter, including thoughts about aspects of your practice that are already strong and those areas in which you will work to improve.)

You've Earned National Board Certification: Now What?

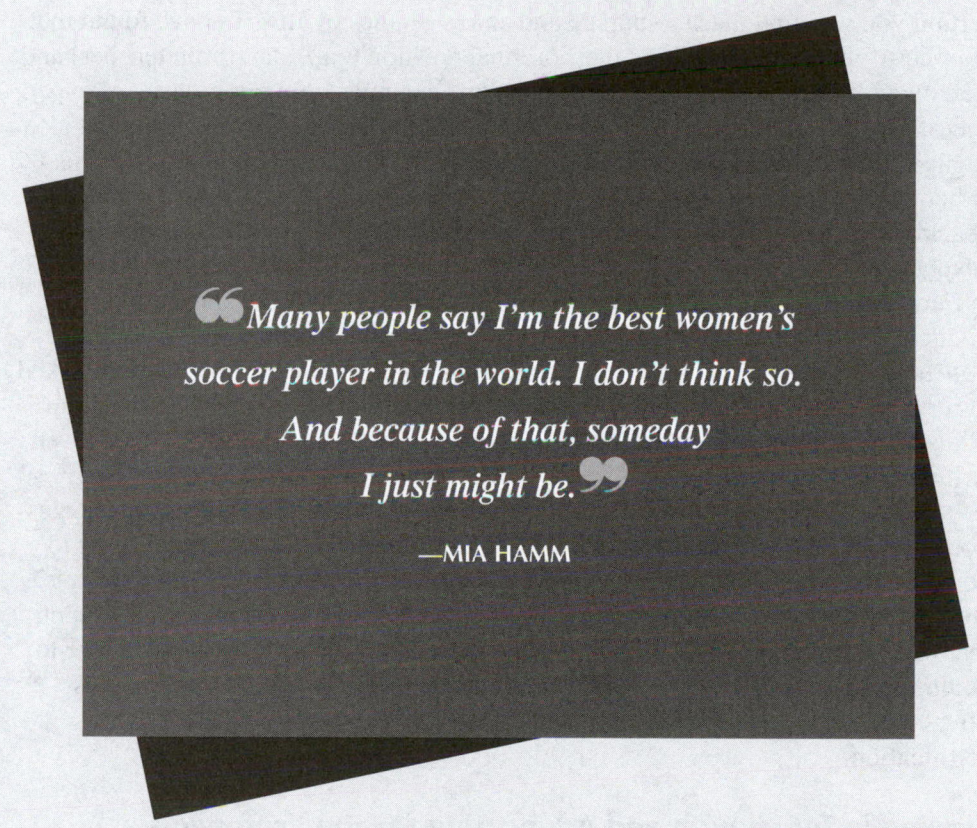

> *Many people say I'm the best women's soccer player in the world. I don't think so. And because of that, someday I just might be.*
>
> —MIA HAMM

Congratulations on earning National Board Certification! You've reached a milestone in your career. This chapter will present you with some ideas for how you might begin (and continue) to share your expertise beyond the bounds of your current assignment as well as build and refine your leadership skills. As a recognized, certified expert in your field you have a responsibility to contribute to the advancement of the education profession—whether locally, nationally, or globally—with the goal of helping others impact student learning in significant ways. You will also find information and ideas about the NBCT renewal process toward the latter part of this chapter.

As the quote at the start of this chapter suggests, having earned the title of National Board Certified Teacher does not exempt one from continuing to exercise humility. As you look to become respected for your leadership, we have found it helpful to keep in mind that you're always a teacher, whether you're working with students, administrators, parents, colleagues, or any stakeholder in education. Even when you're pushing for change, this is best accomplished by respecting (though not necessarily agreeing with) the perspectives of others and actively listening to people's thoughts and concerns.

Each NBCT will travel a different pathway after becoming certified. The specific pathway you travel along is up to you and, with thoughtful choices, we are certain you will find much to pursue and enjoy. Studies of NBCTs have found that after certifying, most remain in their original position (e.g., classroom teacher) and take on additional leadership roles. As just one example from our own set of experiences, Leslee is still teaching kindergarten in a Title 1 school in California but also engages in National Board candidate outreach and support, mentors new teachers in her district, serves as one of the "faculty" of the National Board for Professional Teaching Standards, and lobbies congressional representatives on Capitol Hill to advocate for the teaching profession. Another example is Anthony Cody, an NBCT in Early Adolescence Science from Oakland, California, who has become the science content coach for his school district and writes a regular blog column for *Education Week* that you might have read. Other NBCTs we know have been asked to serve on district curriculum committees, become part of a state education committee, delivered presentations at local and national teacher conferences, and even written books for National Board candidates.

Given the wide range of possibilities, we want to share a few ideas and suggestions to help you think about what might be right for you. It's not about trying to do everything, but about finding what is right for your particular interests, talents, and expertise—and can fit into your busy schedule. And don't miss the section on renewing your certification; if your certificate lapses after 10 years, you'll have to go through the candidate process from scratch to recertify. The renewal process offers a unique opportunity to reflect on your professional growth since initial certification.

Staying in Touch with and Advocating for the Profession

One of the most important (and free) things you can do as an NBCT is to stay in touch with NBPTS through the My Profile portal as well as through services such as NBCT Link (**www.nbctlink.org**) and Smart Brief (**www.smartbrief.com/nbpts**). Be sure to keep your contact information current with NBPTS by logging in to My Profile. This is the only way you can be informed of important events related to your certification (including notices about renewal). Using NBCT Link you will be able to connect with other NBCTs, engage in discussions about education and teaching, learn about NBPTS conferences and events, and stay informed about opportunities to get involved with advocacy for the teaching profession. With Smart Brief, you will receive a daily digest with news stories of interest to teacher leaders. For local involvement, check the NBPTS website to find out if there is an NBPTS network affiliate near you. These are groups of NBCTs who collaboratively work to promote National Board certification, provide candidate support, and advocate for education reforms. Especially if you are one of only a few NBCTs in your school or district, it is helpful to join an affiliate group so you are better connected to the work of other NBCTs. And if you don't find an affiliate within your region, by all means ask NBPTS for their help in starting one.

National Board Candidate Support

One very important role you can take on is that of a support provider for National Board candidates. Check whether your district, county, or state has a system in place for training support providers and matching them with candidates. NBPTS offers its own face-to-face and online training for those interested in becoming "certified" candidate support providers.

⚠ We've provided some ideas for support providers in the Appendix section titled "Guide for Using This Book with Candidates." While there is no one right way to support candidates, there are some "no-no's" to avoid. Be sure to review the ethical guidelines on the NBPTS website before engaging in candidate support.

Involvement with Local Colleges and Universities

Teacher preparation programs, like the one at California State University, Fullerton, seek out NBCTs to serve as cooperating teachers for their teacher candidates. Don't be shy if you're interested in such a role; contact a local teacher preparation program to let them know you're interested in working with their candidates (and check with your principal or district, as they may know of such opportunities, too). With more programs adopting a so-called clinical model for teacher preparation (which focuses on longer and more focused fieldwork) there is a growing need for strong partnerships between teacher preparation programs and K–12 schools, with a particular emphasis on having expert practitioners model best practice (National Council for Accreditation of Teacher Education [NCATE], 2010). In fact, Tara landed her position as a lecturer in secondary education at a local university that was specifically seeking an NBCT to work with its teacher candidates.

Another way to get involved with colleges and universities is as an instructor. Depending on your area(s) of expertise, you might be qualified to teach prerequisite credential courses, methods courses, or even graduate courses. Many programs have courses and even entire programs built on the foundation of the National Board standards. When applying for such work, it's well advised to highlight that you are National Board certified along with pointing out your experience and expertise as an education professional. Most institutions, even if they do not need your services at the moment, will keep your résumé on file in case a need arises in the future.

Professional Organizations

You might (and ought to) be a member of one or more professional organizations and probably know that these nonprofit groups rely on a cadre of volunteers to accomplish much of their work. These organizations can be local, county, regional, state, national, or international. As a local example, in California, the Orange County Mathematics Council (OCMC) relies solely on volunteers who do everything from putting together newsletters, managing information about its over 200 members, organizing events for local teachers, and putting together an annual mathematics field day for elementary students. Taking a national example, the National Council of Teachers of Mathematics (NCTM), with a membership of over 90,000, has a small number of paid staff who handle day-to-day operations but an army of volunteers who review manuscripts for their journals, put together conference programs, and serve on numerous committees vital to the work of the organization. After many years of such service, Mark was elected to NCTM's Board of Directors in 2010 and will serve in that capacity until 2014. Think about organizations, locally and nationally, that represent professionals engaged in the sort of work you do and consider volunteering your time to help with some of the activities they do. Don't forget that NBPTS is one such professional organization with many ways for you to get involved—check the NBPTS website for opportunities. Working within professional organizations is not only very rewarding but is also a great way to network and get new ideas.

Local, State, and National Education Boards and Committees

If you have an interest in education policy, you might learn about local, state, and national boards and committees whose work involves establishing and reviewing policies that impact the work of educators and administrators. Start with your local school district or county office of education website to learn about the decision-making structure with respect to education policy. Opportunities often exist to apply to be considered for service on a committee. Once you've gained experience with such work locally, think about applying for similar work at the state and national level. From the rhetoric we see and hear about education, it's clear that more accomplished, high-impact teachers need to have their voices heard within the policy-making arena. As you think about these opportunities, talk with those who have served in such a role and learn about the application process—what qualities are sought and what is the time commitment required? This is a great way to contribute to shaping education policy that might better reflect the NBPTS standards.

Back to School

Many National Board certified teachers take literally the mantra of being a lifelong learner and enjoy being a student. Our strongest recommendation if you are considering furthering your education is that you do your homework beforehand and find out all you can about the institution you might attend. At the top of your checklist is to be sure it's accredited by a nationally recognized body. If not, the units earned are nontransferrable and any degree earned is not recognized by many employers. Depending on the degree you're pursuing—master's or doctorate—what follows are some tips and questions to ask in your search for one that's just right for you.

Master's Degree

There are a plethora of master's degree programs out there, so you'll want to use some criteria to determine the program that best fits your preferences. Your first decision is about the discipline in which you want to earn a master's degree. Certainly education is an obvious choice, particularly if you want to learn more about teaching and learning. However, you might also consider a content-focused master's degree program as a way to extend your knowledge of a particular subject. This decision is particularly important if you might want to teach college-level courses in the future; most colleges and universities will require that you have a master's degree in the discipline. So, if you want to teach English courses at the local junior or community college, you'll want to earn your master's degree in English. Some universities offer master's programs within a content discipline specifically for teachers (e.g., master's in English for teachers), so be sure to ask whether this option exists. Such programs typically offer a blend of content and pedagogy coursework.

Once you've decided on a discipline, think about how you best learn and the resources you have to support your education. If you learn best through face-to-face interaction, a fully online program may not be the right fit. On the other hand, if you live two hours from campus a distance program might be worth considering. With improvements in technology, online learning has become ubiquitous in the education marketplace. With firsthand knowledge about best practices for online teaching (CSU Fullerton's College of Education offers several online master's degree programs), we want you to be a well-informed, critical consumer so the time and money you invest in your education will be well spent.

Some questions to ask when searching for a master's program include:

- What percentage of faculty are full time and have doctorate degrees or advanced certifcation? For graduate degrees, the best programs will be staffed primarily by full-time faculty with doctorates and instructors with National Board Certification.

- What will the program cost including all fees? There is no correlation between program cost and program quality! Use cost as one criteria, though not the sole criteria.

- How many students are in each course? Research has shown that 25 students or fewer is optimal for online learning.

- What sort of resources and strategies are used to support learning? Whether it's face-to-face or online, you want to find a program that uses a wide range of approaches to engage students in meaningful interactions with one another and with the material being studied.

- What do program graduates think of their experience? Ask for the names and contact information of recent graduates so you can ask them directly about their perception of the quality of the program.

Doctorate Degree

If you are thinking about a doctorate degree, there are additional considerations. The most important of these is your purpose for pursuing the doctorate degree.[1] If you want to move into educational administration, look for a program designed to prepare students for such work. Likewise if your aim is to become a university tenure-track faculty member, you must identify a program that will provide you with the necessary preparation. An excellent way to get suggestions for programs aligned with your goals is to ask someone already doing the sort of work you're considering to share their insights and experiences. If you want to work toward a

---

[1]Note that there are two types of doctorate degrees one might earn in education: the EdD (Doctor of Education) and the PhD (Doctor of Philosophy). In general, EdD programs are more focused on practical application of research and tend to prepare students for educational leadership or policy positions, while PhD programs are more theoretical in nature and prepare students for university and research positions. That said, this distinction is not always correct, so you must investigate each program you are considering to determine whether it is best for your career objectives.

tenure-track faculty position at a college or university, make an appointment to meet with someone who holds such a position. Or if you're contemplating an administrative position at the district level, ask to talk with someone already doing this work. The perspectives of those already in the field are invaluable and will help focus your efforts to identify an appropriate program.

You must be a critical consumer when it comes to deciding on a doctoral program. There are many programs out there but perhaps only a handful that are right for you. Gather as much information as possible about each program you're considering and never be afraid to ask questions of program faculty, candidates, and graduates. Some questions to ask include:

- What percentage of faculty are full time, where were their doctorate degrees earned, and what is the nature of their scholarly activity? For doctoral programs, you will want all faculty to hold full-time tenure-track or tenured positions with degrees earned from respected institutions. In addition, you want faculty who are active scholars and current in their field (e.g., publishing papers, writing books, or presenting at national conferences).

- Who are some faculty members you might want to work with? The nature of a doctoral program is that of a mentorship. You will have a faculty committee that reviews your work and one faculty member who serves as the chair of this group. It is imperative that you identify a program in which there are one or more faculty members whose professional interests are related to your own. A little research now will pay off later.

- How many students are in each cohort? Doctoral programs should be small and personal. A cohort of less than 10 is not unusual, though some may be as large as 20 for core coursework before students break into their areas of specialization.

- What will the program cost including all fees and what sort of financial support is there for doctoral students? At many colleges and universities, doctoral students are called on to teach undergraduate courses or to help with faculty research projects. In return, they often have their tuition and fees reduced or even waived (and sometimes are also paid a modest wage). Larger institutions also have doctoral scholarships for which you might apply.

- What are program completers doing postdegree? Ask for the names and contact information of recent graduates so you can ask them directly about how well the program prepared them to compete for the position they currently hold (or hope to hold).

- Finally, what is the reputation of the program? While some national publications offer program rankings, it is also wise to ask potential future employers what they think about specific institutions. The more opinions you can get, the more likely you will make a well-informed decision.

Renewing Your Certification

The renewal process for NBCTs differs greatly from the original certification process because the objective is different—to verify that you *continue* to be an expert teacher and educational leader. With that in mind, NBPTS will ask that you submit a Profile of Professional Growth (PPG) to document the ways you've grown as a professional and had an ongoing impact on student learning in the years since becoming National Board certified. Based on our experience with renewal, the process is far less intense than the original certification process. Estimates from NBPTS are that the renewal process involves 30 to 40 hours of your time (and energy) as opposed to over 300 hours typically invested in the full certification process. If you've not done so already, be sure to go through the section in the Preface titled "Renewal Candidate." There we direct you to parts of this book helpful to renewal candidates, including some important tips and reminders for you to consider.

At the time of this writing, you may start on the PPG in either your eighth or ninth year of certification. But why wait? Start collecting evidence now so that when the time comes you will already have some materials to work with. Although you do not need to be teaching or working directly with students in order to renew, you will be asked to submit a video in which you are leading a learning activity with a class of students in the same certificate area and age range for which you certified. For this reason, you must have a current, valid teaching credential at the time of renewal. It is important to note that even if you've changed grade levels or content areas since becoming an NBCT, your renewal must focus on your certificate area. And as always, check with NBPTS for any changes to these requirements.

The PPG consists of three components plus a reflection. Table 9.1 gives a quick glance at the organization of the PPG. You will start with identifying a set of four professional growth experiences (PGEs) that you describe in Component 1. There should be a common theme or set of connections among the PGEs that ties them together. The most important idea to keep in mind is that the PGEs must relate to your work as a professional within your certificate area and have a demonstrable connection to student learning. There are also specific parameters for the PGEs, so be sure to read the PPG instructions carefully. At the time of this writing, for example, among the four PGEs you share there must be at least one that demonstrates your advancement in pedagogical and/or content knowledge and another that shows your knowledge and use of technology to support learning. There are specific page limits for each component and the reflection, so be sure to observe those as well.

Just as with the decisions you made about what to use for the portfolio entries you submitted for certification, you want to select PGEs that can be shown to impact student learning, directly or indirectly. In the words of NBPTS, you should identify experiences that "have been ongoing, varied, and complex"

TABLE 9.1 Overview of the Profile of Professional Growth

Component 1	Component 2	Component 3	Reflection
Describe Four Professional Growth Experiences (PGEs) Related to a Common Theme	Choose one PGE from Component 1 and demonstrate how it has impacted student learning. You must include a video recording of yourself teaching students in the same age range and content area as your certificate.	Choose another PGE from Component 1 and explain how your involvement contributed to student learning. You may include video among the forms of evidence. This work may be with students, colleagues, and/or parents.	Within three pages, provide analysis of patterns and connections among the three components, including challenges you face and areas for continued growth and impact on student learning.

(2009, p. 19). From our experience working with renewal candidates, you will have engaged in far more activities and experiences than you're permitted to share—remember, only four PGEs are allowed. It might be helpful to sit down and talk with either a colleague or a candidate support provider to help brainstorm a list of all the possible experiences you might choose from. You might be surprised at some things you've forgotten you were involved with over the past few years! As you pare down your list to select the final four, think about a set of experiences that together paint a picture of you as a professional within your certificate area who strategically seeks out both opportunities for growth and ways to give back. Once you've decided on the PGEs, Component 1 requires that you describe each in turn and provide sample "products" related to each one. See the PPG directions for specific information about what this might look like.

After describing your four PGEs, you must then chose two of these, one each for Components 2 and 3, and provide evidence about how they have informed your work as a professional including a connection—direct or indirect—to student learning. The key is to focus on examples of how each PGE is connected to some ongoing professional activity (e.g., teaching students, leading professional development with colleagues, or publishing an article in a teacher journal).

For Component 2 you must submit a video of yourself teaching students in the same certificate area and age range as the certificate being renewed. See the PPG instructions for specific video criteria. If you do not have a class of your own students, it is permissible to "borrow" a class from a colleague. Having gone this route, Mark recommends you take time before the video recording day to get to know the students and their needs as learners (e.g., maybe substitute for their regular teacher a few times). It is essential that you can provide evidence that your work with these students is clearly connected to a learning outcome based on your knowledge of them and their prior knowledge.

Component 3, based on one of the PGEs not used for Component 2, asks that you provide evidence and reflect on your work with students, colleagues, and/or parents. You have the option to either submit another video or include work samples related to the PGE.

The final piece of the PPG is the reflection. This is a brief (three-page) commentary that addresses the impact of the selected PGEs, discusses how you might tweak them based on your reflections, considers which of the NBPTS standards you find challenging to meet and how you've worked at doing so, and asks you to examine your growth in the years since becoming an NBCT and offer specific characteristics that seem to define your role as an education professional.

We encourage you to review the "Understanding the Evaluation Criteria" section of NBPTS's Profile of Professional Growth document to get a better sense of how your PPG will be evaluated. In addition, it's always a good idea to ask a trusted family member or friend to look through your materials before you pack them up and send them off for review. If you've remained engaged in your certificate area and sustained the professional actions and dispositions that helped you earn certification in the first place, you need not worry too much about renewing (but just a little worrying is OK). While the process of putting together the PPG takes time, it also gives you a chance to step back and reflect more broadly on the work you do—don't forget to pat yourself on the back for being such an amazing educator!

(Use this space to record ideas generated from reading this chapter, including your thoughts about ways to continue your professional growth and share your expertise.)

_____

_____

_____

_____

_____

_____

_____

_____

_____

_____

_____

_____

_____

_____

_____

_____

_____

_____

_____

References

American Board of Medical Specialties. (2009). What board certification means. Retrieved July 20, 2009, from **http://www.abms.org/About_Board_ certification/means.aspx**

Ball, D., & Cohen, D. (1999). Developing practice, developing practioners: Toward a practice-based theory of professional education. In G. Sykes & L. Darling-Hammond (Eds.), *Teaching as the learning profession: Handbook of policy and practice* (pp. 3–32). San Francisco: Jossey-Bass.

Berliner, D. (2004). Describing the behavior and documenting the accomplishments of expert teachers. *Bulletin of Science, Technology, and Society, 24*(3), 200–212.

Berliner, D. C. (1988, February). The development of expertise in pedagogy. Charles W. Hunt Memorial Lecture presented at the annual meeting of the American Association of Colleges for Teacher Education, New Orleans.

Block, P. (1981). *Flawless consulting: A guide to getting your expertise used* (2nd ed.). San Francisco: Pfeiffer.

Bond, L., Smith, T., Baker, W. K., & Hattie, J. A. (2000). *The certification system of the National Board for Professional Teaching Standards: A construct and consequential validity study*. Greensboro: University of North Carolina, Center for Educational Research and Evaluation.

Bransford, J., Brown, A., & Cocking, R. (2000). *How people learn: Brain, mind, experience and school*. Washington, DC: National Academy Press.

Bransford J., Darling-Hammond, L., & LePage, P. (2005). Introduction. In L. Darling-Hammond and J. Bransford (Eds.), *Preparing teachers for a changing world: What teachers should learn and be able to do* (pp. 1–39). San Francisco: Jossey-Bass.

Carnegie Forum on Education and the Economy. (1986). A nation prepared: Teachers for the 21st century. Washington, DC: The Task Force on Teaching as a Profession.

Cohen, C. E., & Rice, J. K. (2005). *National Board certification as professional development: Design and cost*. Washington, DC: The Finance Project. Retrieved July 21, 2009, from **http://www.nbpts.org/UserFiles/File/Complete_Study_ Cohen.pdf**

Eccles, J. S., Wigfield, A., Midgley, C., Reuman, D., Mac Iver, D., & Feldlaufer, H. (1993). Negative effects of traditional middle schools on students' motivation. *The Elementary School Journal, 93*(5), 553–574.

Eccles, J., & Roeser, R. (2009). Schools, academic motivation, and stage-environment fit. In R Lerner & L. Steinberg (Eds.), *Handbook of adolescent psychology* (3rd ed.). Hoboken, NJ: Wiley.

Eccles, J., & Wigfield, A. (1985). Teacher expectations and student motivation. In J. Dusek (Ed.), *Teacher expectancies* (pp. 185–217). Hillsdale, NJ: Earlbaum.

Education Trust. (2005). Gaining traction, gaining ground: How some high schools accelerate learning for struggling students. Retrieved October 5, 2011 from **http://www.edtrust.org/sites/edtrust.org/files/publications/files/GainingTrac- tionGainingGround.pdf**.

Ericsson, K. A., Krampe, R. Th., & Tesch-Romer, C. (1993). The role of deliberate practice in the acquisition of expert performance. *Psychological Review, 100*(3), 363–406.

Ertmer, P., & Newby, T. (1996). The expert learner: Strategic, self-regulated, and reflective. *Instructional Science, 24,* 1–24.

Garmston, R., & Wellman, B. (1999). *The adaptive school: A sourcebook for developing cooperative groups.* Norwood, MA: Christopher-Gordon.

Hakel, M. D., Koenig, J. A., & Elliott, S. W. (Eds.). (2008). *Assessing accomplished teaching: Advanced-level certification programs.* Washington, DC: National Academies Press.

Hamre, B., & Pianta, R. (2005). Can instructional and emotional support in the first-grade classroom make a difference for children at risk of school failure? *Child Development, 76*(5), 949–967.

Hiebert, J., Morris, A. K., Berk, D., & Jansen, A. (2007). Preparing teachers to learn from teaching. *Journal of Teacher Education, 58*(1), 47–61.

Hoffer, E. (1976). *The ordeal of change.* New York: Buccaneer Books.

Hudson, F. M. (1999). *The handbook of coaching: A comprehensive resource guide for managers, executives, consultants, and human resource professionals.* San Francisco: Jossey-Bass.

Jonson, K. (2002). *Being an effective mentor: How to help beginning teachers to succeed.* Thousand Oaks, CA: Corwin Press.

Krull, E., Oras, K., & Sisack, S. (2007). Differences in teachers' comments on classroom events as indicators of their professional development. *Teaching and Teacher Education, 23,* 1038–1050.

Lave, J., & Wenger, E. (1991). *Situated Learning: Legitimate peripheral participation.* Cambridge, UK: Cambridge University Press.

Little, J. W., Gearhart, M., Curry, M., & Kafka, J. (2003). Looking at student work for teacher learning, teacher community, and school reform. *Phi Delta Kappan, 85,* 184–192.

Lord, B. (1994). Teachers' professional development: Critical colleagueship and the role of professional communities. In N. Cobb (Ed.), *The future of education: Perspectives on national standards in education* (pp. 175–204). New York: College Entrance Examination Board.

Lustick, D., & Sykes, G. (2006). National Board Certification as professional development: What are teachers learning? *Education Policy Analysis Archives, 14*(5). Retrieved July 21, 2009, from **http://epaa.asu.edu/epaa/v14n5/**

Marzano, R. (2003). *What works in schools: Translating research into action.* Alexandria, VA: ASCD Press.

National Board for Professional Teaching Standards. (2002). What teachers know and should be able to do. Retrieved July 15, 2009, from **http://www.nbpts.org/UserFiles/File/what_teachers.pdf**

National Board for Professional Teaching Standards. (2008). Guidelines for ethical candidate support. Retrieved July 10, 2011, from **http://www.nbpts.org/userfiles/File/Ethics_Policy_Final_2008(2).pdf**

National Board for Professional Teaching Standards. (2009). *NBCT certification renewal: Profile of professional growth.* Retrieved July 13, 2011, from **http://www.nbpts.org/userfiles/File/Profile_ProfGrowth.pdf**

National Council for Accreditation of Teacher Education. (2010). Transforming teacher education through clinical practice: A national strategy to prepare effective teachers. Retrieved July 1, 2011, from **http://www.ncate.org/LinkClick.aspx?fileticket=zzeiB1OoqPk%3d&tabid=715**

National Research Council. (2000). *How people learn.* Washington, DC: National Academy Press.

National School Reform Faculty. (n.d.). Pocket guide to probing questions. Retrieved from **http://www.nsrfharmony.org/protocol/doc/probing_questions_guide.pdf**

Patterson, K., Grenny, J., McMillan, R., & Switzler, A. (2002). *Crucial conversations: Tools for talking when stakes are high*. New York: McGraw-Hill.

Perkins, D. (1993). Making thinking visible. Seattle: New Horizons for Learning. Retrieved from **http://www.pz.harvard.edu/vt/VisibleThinking_html_files/06_AdditionalResources/MakingThinkingVisible_DP.pdf**

Resnick, M. D., Bearman, P. S., Blum, R. W., Bauman, K. E., Harris, K. M., Jones, J., … Udry, J. R. (1998). Protecting adolescents from harm: Findings from the National Longitudinal Study on Adolescent Health. *Journal of the American Medical Association, 278,* 823–832.

Rodgers, C. (2002a). Defining reflection: Another look at John Dewey and reflective thinking. *Teachers College Record, 104*(4), 842–866.

Rodgers, C. (2002b). Seeing student learning: Teacher change and the role of reflection. *Harvard Educational Review*, *72*(2), 230–253.

Rosaen, C. L., Lundeberg, M., Cooper, M., Fritzen, A., & Terpstra, M. (2008). Noticing noticing: How does investigation of video records change how teachers reflect on their experiences? *Journal of Teacher Education, 59*(4), 347–360.

Santagata, R., Zannoni, C., & Stigler, J. (2007). The role of lesson analysis in pre-service teacher education: An empirical investigation of teacher learning from a virtual video-based field experience. *Journal of Mathematics Teacher Education, 10,* 123–140.

Scardamalia, M., & Bereiter, C. (2006). Knowledge building: Theory, pedagogy, and technology. In K. Sawyer (Ed.), *Cambridge handbook of the learning sciences* (pp. 97–118). New York: Cambridge University Press.

Schon, D. (1983). *The reflective practitioner: How professionals think in action.* New York: Basic Books.

Schunk, D., Pintrich, P., & Meece, J. (2008). *Motivation in education: Theory, research, and applications* (3rd ed.). Upper Saddle River, NJ: Pearson.

Sheldon, S. (2003). Linking school-family-community partnerships in urban elementary schools to student achievement on state tests. *The Urban Review, 35,* 139–165.

Sheldon, S., & Epstein, J. (2005). Involvement counts: Family and community partnerships and mathematics achievement. *Journal of Educational Research*, *98*(4), 196–207.

Shulman, L. (1986). Those who understand: Knowledge growth in teaching. *Educational Researcher, 15*(1), 4–14.

Shulman, L. (1987). Knowledge and teaching: Foundations of the new reform. *Harvard Educational Review, 57*(1), 1–22.

Stigler J., & Hiebert, J. (1999) *The teaching gap: Best ideas from the world's teachers for improving education in the classroom.* New York: Free Press.

Thompson, J., Braaten, M., Windschitl, M., Sjoberg, B., Jones, M., & Martinez, K. (2009). Examining student work: Evidence-based learning for students and teachers. *The Science Teacher, 76*(8), 48–52.

Tschannan-Moran, M. (2003). Fostering organizational citizenship: Transformational leadership and trust. In W. K. Hoy & C. G. Miskel (Eds.), *Studies in leading and organizing schools* (pp. 157–179). Greenwich, CT: Information Age.

Van Es, E., & Sherin, M. (2002). Learning to notice: Scaffolding new teachers' interpretations of classroom interactions. *Journal of Technology and Teacher Education, 10*(4), 571–596.

Van Zee, E., & Minstrell, J. (1997). Using questioning to guide student thinking. *The Journal of the Learning Sciences, 6*(2), 227–269.

Wood, C. (1997). *Yardsticks: Children in the classroom ages 4–14: A resource for parents and teachers.* Greenfield, MA: Northeast Foundation for Children.

Appendix: Providing Candidate Support

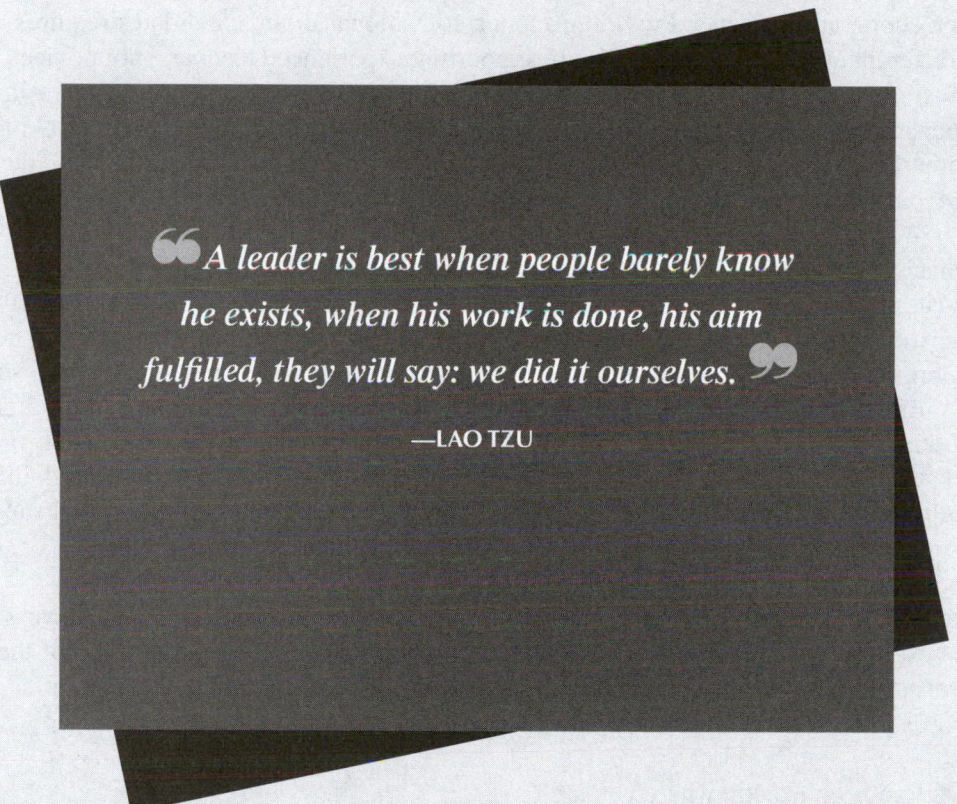

> 66 *A leader is best when people barely know he exists, when his work is done, his aim fulfilled, they will say: we did it ourselves.* 99
>
> —LAO TZU

The work of a skillful candidate support provider, as that of a teacher, requires finding balance. There is a push and pull to providing support. The push comes from asking challenging questions to elicit a candidate's professional growth; the pull comes from asking with sensitivity to the emotions these questions may elicit and the readiness of the candidate to hear and answer these questions. Push too little, and opportunities for growth are missed. Push too much, and opportunities for growth are thwarted. Another pull is that of time and energy demands from the candidate. Without some push back from you, candidate support can become an all-consuming venture. To be an effective (and sane) support provider, you must be clear about your role and about how and when to use your support tools. This Appendix is designed to assist you in striking an appropriate balance in your work.

Please note that the best preparation for providing candidate support is offered by NBPTS through its candidate support provider (CSP) training seminars that you can learn about through the NBPTS website. We can tell you from our firsthand experience going through this training that it's well worth the time you'll invest!

In addition, if it's been awhile since you've worked with any of the NBPTS standards documents, we urge you to read through Chapter 2 in this book (as well as skimming through the other chapters). You might also visit the NBPTS website to review the Five Core Propositions, the Architecture for Accomplished Teaching, and specific certificate standards related to the candidates for whom you're providing support. Be advised, the certificate standards and candidate instructions are routinely reviewed and updated! It's important that you stay current.

The Role of the Support Provider

We recognize that you might have mentored preservice and new teachers or served as a cooperating teacher. Providing support to National Board candidates requires a different approach because you are supporting experienced teachers, not novices. Most importantly, as a candidate support provider you must refrain from expressing your judgment of a candidate's work and instead work to elevate his or her thinking about how well the candidate's practice reflects the National Board standards. The feedback you provide must be through the lens of these standards.

While it may be obvious that the job of a support provider is to provide support, what does that "support" actually look like? What forms can support take? In its candidate support provider training, NBPTS focuses on four forms of support: emotional, logistical, technical, and intellectual. We will provide an overview of each of these (but, again, encourage you to attend the NBPTS CSP training if you've not already done so).

Emotional support, such as cheerleading, is something to be mindful of throughout the certification process. Some candidates can become mired in thoughts of what they are *not* doing well, so helping them focus on and see what they are doing well maintains a professionally healthy perspective. And oftentimes emotional support means simply encouraging the candidate to continue the journey when he or she becomes discouraged or frustrated. Following are some quick one-liners we have found useful in helping candidates redirect in such moments. Sometimes less is best! The less said, the more you are helping the candidate take ownership of the process and move forward in his or her thinking. With that in mind, a few simple words are often enough to help move a candidate forward:

- I've been exactly where you are!
- You *can* do this!
- You are an accomplished teacher; now document that!
- Move on, move forward!
- The bumps in the road are what make you stronger and wiser.
- Persevere!

Support can also be logistical or technical in nature. Setting up an appropriate place and time to work, providing a binder to organize their materials, or volunteering to record their classroom videos are a few examples of this type of support. The extent to which you engage in these activities may depend on the structure of your support program (e.g., one-on-one vs. group; face-to-face vs. online). Additional considerations for logistical and technical support are found later in this Appendix.

The form of support that we find defines most of our work with candidates is intellectual support. This essential work involves supporting candidates as they dig into the videos, the work samples, and the portfolio drafts. We do this mainly by asking questions of candidates. Your role is not to "evaluate" or "fix" their teaching, it is to help them better understand, analyze, and articulate the impact their teaching has on students' learning and achievement. They must figure this out themselves by closely examining their practice. Your job, then, is to ask questions rather than make evaluative statements. By asking questions that help *you* as an outsider understand their practice, candidates build greater understanding of their *own* practice. This is the essence of good candidate support.

We've made this sound a bit simple, but finding the appropriate mixture of support, of push and pull, takes time and practice. The following techniques and tips are ones we have found helpful in working both with individuals and groups of candidates.

Tools for Talking About Teaching

Regardless of the size of the group, there are some dialogue tools you should have in your toolbox from which to strategically draw. We've compiled some useful ones that we use in our work with candidates and with adult learners. You will find a description of each tool and a sample scenario where each is put in action. Mastering the use of these will improve your ability to build trust, push candidates to think more deeply about their work, and avoid some of the common pitfalls when supporting candidates.

Keep in mind that all the tools in the world will be of little use if you've not given attention to establishing and maintaining a safe, trusting environment for your work with candidates. A key component of this is to listen carefully and critically to what candidates are saying, both verbally and nonverbally (e.g., body language). If you're providing support in an online environment, take time to review common rules of "netiquette" so you communicate effectively in that medium. Candidates will feel respected if they know you are tuned in to what they are saying. When engaged in candidate support, set aside any distractions and give the candidates your full attention—they will notice and appreciate this!

Pausing

You may know about wait-time in classrooms. It is just as important with adult learners. Building in and enforcing pauses *before* participants verbalize their thoughts gives everyone time to clarify their thinking and increases the quality of the dialogue. Get in the habit of pausing before you respond to comments or questions. You may find that the first question a candidate asked was not complete, or that not everyone in the group finished speaking. Your job is to encourage constructive dialogue, not stifle or dominate it. Try to hang back, analyze the situation, and see what happens. Oftentimes when working with a group the dialogue will take shape and resolve any issues without your input. Take note of the difference between the two dialogues that follow.

Support provider [SP]: What do you notice?

Candidate 1 [C1]: Well, I saw lots of engaged body language …

SP: Right, many of the students were leaning forward and making eye contact with each other during group work. I also saw them arranging the paper on the desks so that everyone could easily read them instead of one person controlling all the resources. That is evidence for engagement and equity and access.

versus

SP: What do you notice?

C1: Well, I saw lots of engaged body language …

[4-second pause]

Candidate 2 [C2]: Like, they were leaning forward

C1: Right, and looking at each other when they were talking, so you could tell they were actually listening to each other.

C2: So, that would be evidence for "Learning Environment," right?

[3-second pause]

C1: I think I need to look at the Scoring Guide again.

The candidates should be doing the cognitive heavy lifting, not you. Wait them out and see if they can find the evidence in the student work and videos themselves rather than pointing it out for them. One of the most important techniques you will use as a candidate support provider is listening and allowing candidates to learn how to reflect and analyze by doing the work themselves. By hanging back, you demonstrate respect for their expertise and learning. This is just as important when working with one candidate or when providing support online, so be sure to consider how you can step back in these settings to allow space for candidate thinking to occur.

Staying out of the conversation is not the same as tuning out. Closely monitor candidates' words and body language (or emoticons in the online environment) and be prepared to provide guidance when the group stalls or drifts. Reflective tossing, described in the following text, is one way to provide direction without being directive.

Reflective Tossing

The "reflective toss" (Van Zee & Minstrell, 1997) is particularly effective when a candidate is pressing *you* to provide an answer instead of doing his or her own meaning-making. For example:

Candidate: So, should I use this clip, or this other one?

Support provider: Well, I think there is more evidence of the standards in the first clip, so I'd go with that one.

versus

Candidate: So, should I use this clip, or this other one?

Support provider: Hmm. Both clips include evidence, so maybe we should think about the quality, quantity, and types of evidence in each clip. What standards do the portfolio instructions require you to provide evidence for?

In the latter exchange, the support provider uses the reflective toss to put the hard work of analyzing and reflecting back on the candidate, where it belongs. The support provider recognizes this is not his or her portfolio entry and so should not be making any decisions for the candidate. Notice the reflective toss is not "I don't know—what do you think?" The support provider skillfully provides the candidate with some information to inform his or her next move, but it is up to the candidate to analyze the clips and determine what to include in the portfolio.

Probing

But what do you do if after using wait-time and reflective tosses, neither the candidate nor others in the group respond? Resist the temptation to weigh in with an opinion. Instead, try probing to stimulate dialogue. Sometimes you probe to encourage wider participation; sometimes you probe to increase the quality of the dialogue. Let's take a look at both moves.

Drawing participants into the dialogue can be tricky because you do not want to make participants feel anxious, but participation from *all* group members is important for building trust. Probing for participation can take these forms:

- "What do you think, _____?"
- "What do you see, _____?"
- "I'm interested in what _____ may have to say."
- "What's your perspective on this, _____?"

Sometimes, initial contributions to the dialogue can be superficial—a typical pattern for those who are not yet skilled in the art of deep analysis of their teaching. This is where you come in. A strong portfolio entry provides clear, consistent, and convincing evidence, so you will want to gently push participants to clarify vague statements. Vagaries often include people, verbs, comparators, quantifiers, and absolutes (Garmston & Wellman, 1999). Probing for clarity will increase the quality of the analysis and the written entry. Regular use of this tool will create and enforce a norm of "critical colleagueship" (Lord, 1994). This is a regular practice of organized and deliberate investigations where relevant information is acquired and used to construct sound arguments and flimsy reasoning is rejected when faced with countervailing evidence.

Probing for clarification can take these forms:

- "Which students, specifically?"
- "*All* parents?"
- "How do you know when they understand, exactly?"
- "I want to better understand what you mean by 'engaged.'"
- "All right, so, where do you see that in the video?"
- "That's an interesting point. Can you show me where you see that in the work sample?"
- "I'd like to hear more about what you mean by 'better.' Better than what, exactly?"
- "In what ways is this group *slower*? Can you explain more about that?"
- "I heard you say that you *have to* teach this. What would happen if you didn't?"

Tone and timing can be important when probing. Keep your tone neutral and nonaggressive. Often, setting up a probe by first paraphrasing can also decrease the candidate's defensiveness by marking the probe as an attempt to understand rather than a critique. The next section describes how to use paraphrasing effectively.

Paraphrasing

Paraphrasing, or revoicing, is taking what a participant said or wrote and putting what you think it means in your own words. It must be done in a way that frames your rephrasing as an attempt to clarify and better understand the participant's perspective. Using this tool sends the message that you are listening and that you care enough about what is being said to try to make meaning of it. Again, you are attending to what the candidate is saying. This builds trust and group comprehension and helps move the analysis along (Garmston & Wellman, 1999; Patterson et al., 2002).

Paraphrasing can take these forms:

- "So, you're saying that this student error is an example of …?"
- "So, you're thinking when the student gives a thumbs up, that means … ?"
- "So, in this clip you want us to look for evidence of … ?"
- "You're feeling that teaching the lesson on multiplication first would be more effective then?"
- "You're suggesting that critical thinking looks like… . Is that right?"

As with probing, tone is important when paraphrasing. Stay calm and neutral to maintain a safe environment for the work. Do not react emotionally if the accuracy of your paraphrase is rejected. One of the purposes for paraphrasing is to illuminate thought. By talking through ideas, putting them into words, and hearing how they are interpreted by others, one gains greater insight to and clarity of one's thoughts. It is a natural and normal part of this work, but it may take some getting used to for both support provider and candidate.

> 66 *We are a deeply influential profession. Our level of practice matters—and the public's perception of our level of practice matters, too.*
>
> *That is why I coach.* 99
>
> —NBCT, LITERACY: READING–LANGUAGE ARTS

Giving Feedback

The bulk of your work should be spent encouraging candidates to talk, but the content and delivery of your verbal contributions are important. Peter Block, author of *Flawless Consulting* (1981), recommends using language that is descriptive, focused, specific, brief, and simple when giving feedback. Rely on facts rather than opinions. Focus on what is controllable and important. Be thoughtful with your delivery, but not wishy-washy; this makes you look disingenuous and hides what is likely critical information. Stay clear about the big picture in your work. Let go of a point if it is not central to the objective you are trying to accomplish. Also be prepared to back off if it is clear that the receiver of the feedback is not ready to accept your comments. Leave it for the receiver to mull over in his or her own time frame.

Here are some contrasting examples of ineffective versus effective feedback:

- "This is probably a bad idea, but what if you did the activity before the lecture, maybe?" [ineffective: too wishy-washy]

versus

- "What do you think would happen if you did the activity before the lecture?" [effective]

- "I think this is really great, and the kids seem to have had fun with this, but maybe you should think about ..." [ineffective: uses judgmental language and hides intentions]

versus

- "Comparing what you described to the standards, I'm not clear on how this activity serves as evidence for finding patterns. Can you clarify and explain your reasoning as you might do for the assessors?" [effective]

- "I don't get it." [ineffective: vague]

versus

- "I want to understand how these two assignments build on the development of writing craft. Help me see this from your perspective." [effective]

- "That's not going to work; I've tried it." [ineffective: aggressive, dismissive, and prescriptive]

versus

- "I encountered a problem with too many students getting stuck at the second step when I tried it. What are some ways you can address that in your design?" [effective]

Additional tips on responding to particularly challenging candidate situations are described later in the "Common Candidate Challenges" section of this Appendix.

Keep in mind that some amount of tension, termed *productive disequilibrium* (Lord, 1994), is healthy in a safe and professional environment. Modeling how to paraphrase, probe, and provide feedback respectfully in your interactions with candidates will help create and maintain this important safe space. The next section describes specific strategies for building and maintaining productive collaborative pairs and groups.

Building and Maintaining a Safe and Productive Environment

So far, we've advocated for the need to be mindful of dominating the dialogue for a few reasons. First, the candidates should be the ones learning about their craft in this process, so they need to have the space to grow in their own time. Second, if you want to be heard, you must also demonstrate that you can listen attentively. Much of your work is simply to be an ear, not a mouthpiece. This is not your journey; you are the guide, not the traveler.

Here is the caveat. If trust, safety, or productivity is in danger, don't wait—intervene. Trust and safety are difficult to build up and even more difficult to recover when damaged. Work hard to build a positive environment and remain vigilant against threats to these aspects of your community or partnership. What follows are some suggestions for building and maintaining trust, safety, and productivity.

Organizing the Meeting Space

As mentioned earlier, it is important for all participants to contribute in order to build a sense of trust. For face-to-face groups, the arrangement of people and furniture in the meeting space definitely influences the sense of community in the group or partnership, so it warrants attention. Garmston and Wellman (1999) provide some tips for organizing meeting space in *The Adaptive School*. Try to face the meeting away from doors or windows to limit distractions. If possible, keep chairs close together to reduce the likelihood of disengagement. If working with a group, be sure to seat everyone so they can easily see and hear each other as well as any easels or screens for viewing video. Remove empty chairs to encourage a sense of belongingness. This also makes it more awkward for those who arrive late! For groups that meet frequently, encourage participants to sit next to different people each time to expand perspectives and reduce sidebar conversations. It is also important to negotiate and enforce some norms for how the group will function. Considerations for the construction of norms are in the following section.

Clarifying the Ground Rules

Before you enter into a professional support relationship with candidates, it is important to make clear what they can expect of you and what you expect of them. The first step is to review with candidates the NBPTS ethical guidelines. These both inform and constrain the work of the candidate and the support provider.

Next it's time to set some boundaries and expectations for your relationship with candidates. Decide if you will be available via phone, email, face-to-face, or some combination of the three. Determine the frequency and duration of meetings and turnaround times to respond to emails and phone messages. Specify how long it will take you to provide feedback on written work and how many times you will read an entry. Consider asking candidates about their expectations and concerns to be sure they are either well aligned with the support you will provide or in need of clarification.

Last, but certainly not least, you will want to clarify norms for how the group or partnership will function during meetings. Commitments to be on time, come prepared, contribute, avoid engaging in side conversations, and maintain positive presuppositions are common group norms. For online support, remind everyone of proper etiquette when communicating through text (search for "netiquette" if you want to learn more about this). For instance, sarcasm does not translate well when sent in a typed response. Once norms are determined, record them, distribute them, and revisit them regularly.

Following a Plan

Clarify the goal and a time limit for each meeting and stick to them. Start on time and end on time. Remind participants of the goals at the start of each meeting and end with a clear outline of what is to be done before the next meeting. Using a protocol can help participants stay on task and focused on the work. This limits defensive talk and over- and under-participation by group members, and maintains the emphasis on key aspects of the analysis. The National School Reform Faculty has many protocols and directions for their use on its website at **www.nsrfharmony.org**. Even with a protocol, there will be times when you will need to intervene to refocus the group. The next section describes some techniques for redirecting.

Maintaining Productivity by Redirecting

Anticipate having to redirect the conversation to stay on topic and focused on evidence rather than unsubstantiated claims or opinions. Without occasional redirecting, collegial groups can drift into gripe sessions or soapboxing. A little bit of venting is OK, but participants tend to become frustrated when too much time is consumed with unproductive grumbling. Remind candidates to explain their teaching circumstances, not complain about them. Gently guide them back to the topics at hand using the standards as the lens for focusing the work.

Redirecting could look like this:

"OK, but what do the portfolio instructions say?"

"Mmm hmm, and how does this relate to …?"

"Good observation, but I remember we agreed to focus on looking for evidence of _____ right now, so let's return to that."

"So how could you word that more proactively?"

Take a moment to look back at the exchange between Maria, Bill and Lisa in Chapter 5 to see some of these tools you've read about so far in action. Maria, the candidate support provider, asks Bill to situate the clip by providing some background about the lesson (line 1). She then helps focus Bill and Lisa to look for evidence by reminding them about the Evidence Guide (line 12). After watching the clip, she starts with Lisa, asking her an open question, "What do you notice?" (line 90). Maria stands back while Bill answers Lisa's questions about the clip, not speaking again until line 113. Maria is allowing the candidates to analyze the clip together, but intervenes when she senses they are starting to drift. She redirects them back to evidence of student learning in line 113 and again at line 125. Maria reads directly from the goal that Bill stated and presses him on evidence for that learning goal.

Had Maria not intervened at these points, it is possible Bill and Lisa would not have addressed the issue Maria sees: Students in the clip demonstrated a simple understanding of the locations of the ancient civilizations, but evidence of their knowledge about how humans adapted to a variety of environments is lacking. Maria skillfully directs attention to this issue without overtly pointing it out. She allows the candidates to arrive at this conclusion on their own. Maria presses and redirects on a few more occasions (lines 133, 149, 155, and 162). While she asks many questions, she is careful to not step in with answers. That work is left up to Bill and Lisa. In the entire exchange between this trio, Maria speaks only 9 times compared to Bill's 15 and Lisa's 14. But the few times she does speak are at critical junctures—she is able to redirect and focus the candidates on the analysis of the student learning using the standards as a guide, making this time highly productive for both Bill and Lisa.

Keeping the time you spend with candidates highly productive and focused on the work at hand builds trust that time will not be wasted and promotes a sense of accomplishment. This type of positive environment can make the hard work exhilarating and something to look forward to. It takes work to maintain this atmosphere. The following section describes some potential threats to maintaining a safe environment and ways to avoid these, and, when necessary, strategies to repair relationships.

Maintaining the Environment

You should constantly be on the lookout for signs of distress in your candidates. Patterson and colleagues (2002), in *Crucial Conversations*, identify and describe several "safety problems" related to working with individuals who have made themselves vulnerable for the sake of professional growth. These are found in Table A.1.

Once you identify these behaviors, what do you do about them? Recognize that they are likely caused by fear. A candidate may be emotionally defending against

TABLE A.1 Safety Problems That Can Undermine Collaborative Work Environments

Safety Problem	Definition	Examples of Candidate Remarks
Masking	Understating or selectively showing true opinions. Sarcasm, sugarcoating, and couching are some of the more popular forms.	"Oh, yeah. The students will *love* that." "Whatever." "Sure that works with *honors* students."
Avoiding	Involves steering completely away from sensitive subjects.	"I know she still has some difficulty with subject–verb agreement, but she really had fun with this assignment."
Withdrawing	Pulling out of a conversation altogether, usually by exiting the conversation or the room.	"Excuse me for a moment; I have to check on something." "Can we talk about this later?"
Controlling	Coercing others to your way of thinking by forcing your views on others or dominating the conversation. Can include cutting off others, overstating facts, speaking in absolutes, changing subjects, or using directive questions to control the conversation.	"Everyone knows that scripted curricula never work!" "All kids love the computer. It's totally engaging. They'd spend all day on it if I let them." "There's no way to cover all that content in one semester."
Labeling	Putting a label on people or ideas so you can dismiss them under a general stereotype or category.	"All charter schools do is steal all the bright students out of my class. They aren't any more effective—they've just got the right kids." "Well, he's an administrator; what does he know?"
Attacking	Self-explanatory. Tactics include belittling and threatening.	"Maybe being mediocre is OK for you, but not for me."

Source: Modeled after Patterson et al. (2002), pp. 51–54.

confronting a reality he or she would rather avoid. Be sensitive but firm and consistent in calling these out, especially the last three that are more aggressive or antagonistic. Left unchecked these behaviors will eat away at the sense of safety and trust in your group. Be direct about it; name the behavior, apologize if necessary, and immediately work to rebuild trust by reestablishing your common purpose.

Consider this interaction:

Jacob [support provider]: Alex, you seem frustrated.

Alex [candidate]: No, I'm not.

Jacob: Your body language makes me think that you are. You pushed away from the table and frowned. [5-second pause] What's going on?

Alex: This is hard, OK? I don't have access to the resources everyone else does, and I don't work with motivated kids! All I hear is that there's no evidence in my clip, and that I'm a crummy teacher! I'm doing the best that I can with what I have.

Jacob: I don't recall hearing anyone say "you're a crummy teacher," Alex. I don't want to give you that impression. I'm here to help you do your best. If I pushed too hard, too quickly, I'm sorry. Do you want to work on documenting your areas of accomplishment and identifying your areas of growth together?

Alex's behavior can be caustic if it is not addressed. Jacob called it out, identified what was motivating it, and moved to address it. Jacob did not back off the need for Alex to identify some areas for growth, but he was able to repair damage to the relationship and to Alex's ego. By demonstrating humility and sensitivity to Alex, Jacob restored trust and safety with the entire group.

Make no mistake: this is challenging work. Do not assume that teachers automatically know how to collaborate effectively. Part of your role is to establish a productive environment by communicating the values of critical colleagueship, modeling them in your interactions, and holding group members accountable to them. You likely will have to be more overtly involved in the managing of the group discussion early on, but as the group builds trust and gains experience and familiarity with this work and the specific ways to go about it, your role will become less and less pronounced.

Common Candidate Challenges

Now that you are familiar with some tools, here are some common challenges where you can put them into practice. None are insurmountable, but it's always helpful to think about how you might respond before the situation presents itself.

The more you work with candidates, the more skilled you will become at supporting them and assisting them in navigating their journey. At the same time you will also encounter a number of candidates with diverse personalities, needs, and situations. You will want to strategically use your tools for candidate support as you work with candidates, whatever the format of your support program. Be aware that the format impacts not just how you support candidates, but also their reactions and interactions.

With such a rigorous certification process, candidates often feel exposed or challenged in regard to their professional practice in ways that are new and uncomfortable. As accomplished teachers, many are accustomed to being recognized as effective and oftentimes revered by administration, parents, and peers. Thus analyzing one's practice in such an in-depth manner, against such high standards, may bring new and different emotions and reactions to the forefront. Sometimes, these emotions and reactions are not productive, so you will want to quickly intervene and get your candidate(s) back on track!

What follows are four candidate situations we've encountered and some bulleted suggestions for responding to them. These are not meant to cast candidates negatively but to acknowledge the sort of encounters you might have when working with professionals in what can be a very stressful process.

The Defensive Candidate

The defensive candidate is one who may feel the need to defend his or her teaching, writing, comments, and thoughts. Addressing this will require not just intellectual support, but use of your people skills as you will need to read the candidate to know exactly why he or she may be exhibiting defensive behaviors. This candidate reacts negatively to questioning. Rather than explaining practice, he or she tends to argue. The candidate often acts out in aggressive or demonstrative ways. The behavior of this type of candidate often makes others feel unsafe. When responding:

- Do not take it personally.
- Determine what he or she is reacting to and why. It may be because you identified a real problem.

- Identify the resistance, name it, and wait for a response.
- Stick with facts and be brief.
- Clarify your intentions and correct any misunderstandings if needed.
- Remind him or her to make *positive* rather than negative presuppositions—the candidate is not under attack.
- Apologize if necessary and move to rebuild the relationship by reminding the candidate of a common goal.

  (Consult the previous interaction between Alex and Jacob as an example.)

The Discouraged Candidate

The discouraged candidate is ready to give up and throw in the towel. This candidate may also react negatively to questioning. But, unlike the defensive candidate, the discouraged candidate directs his or her negativity inward. The candidate may express feelings of not being "good enough." This is where you will want to be the cheerleader! When responding:

- Remind the candidate to make positive rather than negative presuppositions— the point is not to make him or her feel ineffective.
- Encourage the candidate to find the high rather than the low points. But be wary of the temptation to exaggerate his or her virtues in an effort to make the candidate feel better. It is disingenuous and will undermine trust.
- Remind the candidate he or she is already an accomplished teacher, but just needs to identify and analyze the evidence of his or her impact.
- Tell the candidate he or she is not alone; share that we have all been discouraged.
- Acknowledge the rigor of the work. If this process was easy, anyone could do it and it wouldn't be as prestigious!

The Overwhelmed Candidate

The overwhelmed candidate simply has too much on his or her plate. This is a very common characteristic of candidates. They are overwhelmed not just with the certification process but with the combined pressures of professional obligations and their personal lives. The situation sometimes feels insurmountable. In addressing this, you may need to dig into your toolbox and use a range of strategies to provide intellectual, logistical, technical, and emotional support in addition to your people skills. This candidate is like the discouraged candidate in that he or she may express the desire to quit, but for different reasons. As opposed to lacking confidence in his or her teaching, the source of the overwhelmed candidate's struggle may be due to lack of organization, lack of time, or an inability to focus and meet deadlines. You must diagnose the problem before intervening. When responding:

- Help the candidate break down his or her tasks into smaller ones that can be readily completed to build confidence and momentum.
- Encourage the candidate to redirect his or her focus by prioritizing tasks and organizing the candidate's time.
- If experiencing difficulty starting to write, advise the candidate to begin by typing the portfolio prompts into a document so he or she isn't looking at a blank

page. The candidate can then start bulleting the responses and going back later to convert these into sentences.

- When truly blocked on a particular entry, encourage the candidate to set it aside for now and move on to another one.

The Misguided Candidate

The misguided candidate may be misguided, misinformed, or simply not yet where he or she needs to be with the process of certification and what it means to engage an in-depth analysis of one's professional practice. Again, all your candidate support provider tools may be needed to guide this candidate back to the path to ensure a successful journey. This candidate loses sight (or in some cases, never had sight) of the standards or portfolio instructions. When responding:

- Remind the candidate of the standards and portfolio questions. Encourage the candidate to think through what each standard means to him or her. Ask the candidate to think about what it looks like and sounds like in his or her practice.
- Reiterate that candidates often do not certify because they do not respond to the questions posed in the portfolio directions.
- Resist the temptation to tell the misguided candidate how he or she should interpret the standards. You are neither the instructor nor his or her mentor. Instead, ask probing questions to help the candidate clarify his or her thinking and analysis.

Now that you have some exposure to thinking about your work as a support provider, it's time to consider how to use this book with candidates. While we would love for you to read it cover-to-cover and develop your own game plan, we know you're a busy professional who might appreciate the following suggestions as a starting point.

Guide for Using this Book with Candidates

We've designed this book so that candidates can use it on their own, but as support providers we recognize the value an external, objective pair of ears and eyes can provide. It is well known that simply talking through ideas with another person can greatly clarify thought. With that in mind, we've included this Appendix to help support providers who are working with candidates to use this resource to its fullest. All the tools and techniques we've described in the text have been tried and tested by us, and we are thankful for the opportunity to share our experience with you. We care deeply about educators, the profession of education, and the role of National Board Certification in providing an avenue for professionals to both grow as educators and earn recognition for their expert practice.

Chapter 1: Introduction to National Board Certification

This book is organized such that all types of candidate (*Take One!,* full certification, advanced, and renewal) will be able to find information relevant to the activities in which they will be engaged. This first chapter serves to provide an overview of NBPTS and the National Board Certification process. It is useful for you to familiarize yourself with the text, but keep in mind you are not an instructor who is expected to be an "expert" on the content and the text. As a facilitator, you do not have that responsibility.

Chapter 2: Understanding the Standards

This chapter provides an overview of the Five Core Propositions and the Architecture of Accomplished Teaching (and our alternate model titled The Cycle of High-Impact Teaching). Early in our support careers, so many candidates would come to us with entry drafts without having taken the time to read and unpack the standards. If the purpose of the portfolio entries is to determine how well a candidate puts the National Board standards into practice, it only makes sense to invest in deeply understanding the standards. The candidates may be anxious to start planning, analyzing, and writing, but it is vital that you emphasize the need for them to make sense of these standards. This investment will reap benefits later.

Although our text provides a review of the Five Core Propositions and the Architecture of Accomplished Teaching, it is not intended to replace reading the documents provided by NBPTS. After each overview of one of the core propositions, there are prompts in bold. Use these to start a conversation with the candidate about what each looks like and sounds like in practice. If you were to go into the classroom of a National Board Certified Teacher, what would you see and hear the teacher doing and saying? What would you see and hear the students doing and saying?

Once you've unpacked the core propositions, tackle the Architecture of Accomplished Teaching. A description can be found in the portfolio instructions. If our Cycle of High-Impact Teaching is easier to understand and talk about, use that model. Every candidate is different, so use what resonates most with them.

Candidates should read, reread, and annotate their certificate standards. Again, as a facilitator it is not your responsibility to be an expert on anyone's standards. Even if the candidate is pursuing the same certificate you may have certified in (if you are an NBCT yourself), be aware that the standards change. Skim the standards of your candidates, but direct all questions back to the NBPTS documents. It is not your job to interpret them, but it is your job to press for clarity when needed.

Use Table 2.2 to help candidates make sense of and connect the Five Core Propositions and standards with their practice.

Chapter 3: Getting Started

This chapter provides some suggestions for getting started on the process. It may be useful to use this as a way to check in with candidates at the beginning of their journey. Help organize and set timelines, but remember it is not your responsibility to accomplish these tasks. If the candidates do not meet the targets they set, remind them of the consequences and help them problem solve to get back on track. In the end it is up to them to complete this process.

We've found it useful to individually check in with candidates every time we meet (either online or face-to-face). Knowing they will have to verbalize what they accomplished since the previous meeting motivates some candidates to stay productive. Sometimes meetings with candidates can turn into gripe sessions. Candidates need to be able to release pent up emotions, but do not let this go on for too long. Redirect and move forward, particularly if you are working with a group. You owe it to all members of the group to make the support session worthwhile.

Encourage candidates to plan out the entries using the Entry Planning Worksheet (Table 3.1). This tool helps them plan out their year and assists them in determining which lessons or assignments are likely to provide the best evidence for each entry. Since the National Board Certification process is likely new territory for most candidates, it is important to help them be explicit about their planning as it relates to each entry. Ideally, they should come up with multiple instructional sequences, lessons, or assignments for each entry; if one does not work out as well as they planned, they will have a backup. The danger of not mapping out a plan early in the cycle is that some candidates start to run out of time and options as the portfolio deadline approaches. Since a candidate cannot use the same lesson or learning sequence for two entries, it can become a problem if he or she has two entries to complete in the last four weeks.

Candidates often have questions about the portfolio instructions. Rely on the NBPTS documents, but encourage candidates to make their own determinations and, when in doubt, go to the NBPTS website or call 1-800-22-TEACH. Some candidates may ask which lesson, accomplishment, or work sample would be best for an entry. This is not your portfolio, so resist the temptation to provide an opinion. Instead, to help candidates make their own decisions, use your knowledge of the standards established by NBPTS to ask questions about how each piece of evidence relates to these standards.

Chapter 4: Thinking, Dialoguing, and Writing About Teaching

This chapter provides tips for analyzing and reflecting on teaching. Be familiar with these tips, as you may want to direct candidates back to them when they are stuck or are engaging in unproductive analysis and reflection.

At this point, candidates will likely start producing written drafts of their portfolio entries. When reading entries keep the following in mind:

- Remind candidates that as a facilitator you must follow the ethical guidelines for candidate support from NBPTS. As such you will *not* be keeping a file of their portfolio entries or videos they submit to you for review, nor will you be sharing their work with anyone. If providing support in a group, encourage candidates to bring hard copies and collect all copies at the end of each meeting. And caution them about sharing work that includes their candidate ID number.

- Insist that candidates include the portfolio instructions, the standards overview, and the portfolio entry scoring rubric for any entry they'd like you to look over. Your ability to provide useful feedback is curtailed without these supporting documents.

- Set a limit on the number of times you will read an entry, both for your sanity and their independence. Most candidate support providers make it a policy to read candidate entries only once. Encourage candidates to find a reading buddy who will be their first reader.

- You are not an editor, so do not feel compelled to correct grammar, spelling, and the like. They aren't scored on that anyway! Do read for evidence of the standards. Probe and question to improve the focus, clarity, and coherence of the claims they are making about their teaching.

Chapter 5: Looking for Evidence of the Standards

This chapter focuses specifically on evidence. Encourage candidates to use the Evidence Analysis Guide tool (Figure 4.1) to help identify the presence of specific evidence of learning in videos and student work samples. Remind candidates to keep the prompts in the horizontal arrow in mind so their argument is coherent. The stated learning goal, the evidence showing that goal was met, the instruction that contributed to the evidence, and any modifications should all be linked. It may be helpful to look over a video or piece of student work several times, looking for evidence of different standards each time. Again, your role is to probe and question to help candidates paint a clear, consistent, and convincing picture of high-impact teaching.

Chapter 6: Sending Your Portfolio: Packing the Box

This chapter provides tips for packing completed portfolio entries, supporting documents, and forms. The best source of guidance is the directions provided by NBPTS. As with the portfolio writing instructions, it is not your responsibility to be the expert. Refer candidates to the instructions or 1-800-22-TEACH. Completing and submitting the portfolio is reason to celebrate! We often mark the occasion of sending off the box with a small token (a baggie of gold-colored paper clips, a handwritten card, or a celebratory get-together). Regardless of the eventual outcome, each candidate who completes the portfolio has accomplished something few educators ever attempt. This is worth acknowledging!

Chapter 7: Preparing for the Assessment Center

This chapter provides some guidance on how to prepare for assessment center exercises including mock assessments, study tips, and test day pointers. The six assessment center exercises comprise 40 percent of candidates' overall scores, and you want to help them prepare well for these. What you'll want to emphasize to candidates is the need to adequately prepare for the assessment center by reviewing the Scoring Guide for their certificate area and identifying specific content and/or pedagogical topics with which they might be less familiar or confident. In our work with candidates, we hold a timed practice session where candidates complete responses to two of the retired prompts provided by NBPTS. Providing candidates with time to dialogue with one another after the mock assessment session is often very helpful for candidates. This allows us to discuss test taking tips such as pacing and answering all parts of the prompts.

Chapter 8: Planning for Score Release

This chapter is an at-a-glance look at the Score Report and common questions about scoring. It is important to touch base with the candidates you've supported *before* scores are released to let them know you're still there for them, no matter the outcome revealed by the score report! Encourage them to let you know either way whether they achieved certification or not. We provide a quick overview of how the total score is calculated from the raw scores, so you might want to review this. For those who did not certify, be prepared to be their cheerleader and share with them information about becoming a retake candidate (see "How to Use This Book" in the Preface for ideas). The important thing to keep in mind is that each candidate processes the score report in his or her own way; particularly for those who do not certify, it may take some longer than others before they are comfortable talking with you about next steps. Finally, if a candidate wants to question the integrity of the scoring process (e.g., "Why did I get this score?") refer him or her to 1-800-22-TEACH. You were not involved with scoring the work.

Chapter 9: You've Earned National Board Certification: Now What?

This chapter focuses on opportunities for NBCTs to both continue their professional growth in supporting student learning and to expand their involvement with the broader profession. Some of these ideas might be pertinent to you as a support provider as well. Once you learn that a candidate has achieved certification, after you let out a big *hooray*, you'll want to help the candidate think about what he or she might do next. This includes looking ahead to certificate renewal.

In Closing

Supporting National Board candidates is challenging and rewarding work. Assisting one teacher will improve the educational experiences of countless students. But, like teaching, honing this skill also takes time and deliberate practice. Berliner's (1988) research on teacher expertise indicates that it takes seven years for teacher learning curves to begin to flatten out. Ericsson, Krampe, and Tesch-Romer (1993), in their research on the 10,000-hour rule popularized by Malcom Gladwell in *Outliers*, reinforces this theory. Our point is to be patient not only with the candidates you support, but also with yourself. Prepare yourself for each support meeting by reviewing resources such as this book and NBPTS materials, and take time to reflect on how things went afterward. Sharing best practices (and occasional frustrations) with other support providers is also beneficial, both mentally and strategically, to your own professional growth.

We've enjoyed sharing what we've learned about candidate support with you and thank you for your dedication to teachers and to students and their learning. Keep working and learning. Remember: "In times of change, the *learners* will inherit the world, while the *knowers* remain well-prepared for a world that no longer exists" (Hoffer, 1976).

We want to leave you with some well-worn utterances we use to both break the monotony of support sessions and remind candidates, repeatedly, of what they're aiming for. Even though this might seem a more appropriate strategy for the younger students you might work with, adult learners are often not so different. We guarantee that you will get a lot of mileage with these one-liners by generously sprinkling them throughout your sessions. Enjoy!

- What is the impact on student learning?
- Have you read *all* the directions?
- Are you writing your entries through the lens of your certificate standards?
- *So what!* Where is the evidence? Why is it significant?
- Paint the picture!
- Talk to me. Think out loud!

Additional Resources

Garmston, R., & Wellman, B. (1999). *The adaptive school: A sourcebook for developing cooperative groups*. Norwood, MA: Christopher-Gordon.

Patterson, K., Grenny, J., McMillan, R., & Switzler, A. (2002). *Crucial conversations: Tools for talking when stakes are high*. New York: McGraw-Hill.

Rudney, G. L., & Guillaume, A. M. (2003). *Maximum mentoring: An action guide for teacher trainers and cooperating teachers*. Thousand Oaks, CA: Corwin Press.

Schulman, J. H., & Sato, M. (2006). *Mentoring teachers toward excellence: Supporting and developing highly qualified teachers*. San Francisco: Jossey-Bass.

Thompson, J. (n.d.). Mentoring tools for ambitious science teaching. Retrieved from **http://sites.education.washington.edu/mentorsci/**.

Van Es, E. (2010, January/February). A framework for facilitating productive discussions in video clubs. *Educational Technology,* 8–12.

Name Index

Subject Index

Violence, 20
Visitor, 55

W. *See* Weighting factor
Wait-time, 107–108
Weighting factor (W), 88
Wiki, 77
Writing
    analytic, 46
    for assessment center exercises, 80–81
    descriptive, 45

about evidence, 58, 67–68, 121
mechanics, 72
to National Board standards, 58
passive and active, 58–60
reflection and, 44–45
reflective, 46–47

*Yardsticks: Children in the Classroom
    Ages 4–14: A Resource for Parents
    and Teachers* (Wood), 79